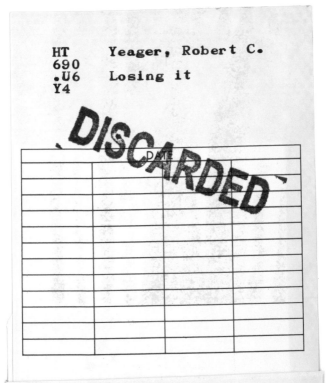

Losing It

Losing It

THE ECONOMIC FALL OF THE

MIDDLE CLASS

Robert C. Yeager

McGRAW-HILL BOOK COMPANY   *New York*

St. Louis   San Francisco   Düsseldorf   Mexico   Toronto

For Don and Johnny

1 2 3 4 5 6 7 8 9 0 B P B P 8 7 6 5 4 3 2 1 0

Library of Congress Cataloging in Publication Data

Yeager, Robert C
Losing it.
1. Middle classes—United States—Case studies.
2. United States—Economic conditions—1961-
I. Title.
HT690.U6Y4   330.973'092'0880622   80-16679
ISBN 0-07-072256-0

Book design by Anita Walker Scott.

The author gratefully acknowledges permission from the following publishers for brief quotations from copyrighted works:
Harcourt Brace Jovanovich, Inc., for the quotation from *1984* by George Orwell on pages 127–128; © copyright 1949 by Harcourt Brace Jovanovich, Inc. Harper & Row, Publishers, Inc., for the quotation from *Brave New World* by Aldous Huxley on page 132; © copyright 1932, 1946 by Aldous Huxley.

Published in association with
SAN FRANCISCO BOOK COMPANY.

Contents

Oh, money, money, money, money,
when will I make the grade?
I'm so broke that a dollar bill
looks big as a window shade.

> from "Empty Pockets Blues"
> by Pete Seeger and Lee Hays

Preface

This is meant to be a small and simple book about the problems of our economy and how they are affecting ordinary Americans. Its most important contributors are some two dozen "Middletown"* families willing to open their homes to a journalist who, armed with note pad and tape recorder, tried to capture the nature of their financial struggles and, more important, how they felt about them.

Only a handful of the interviews could be used at length, but I have attempted to preserve portions of the others in the "Newsreel" sections where often they helped emphasize and illustrate points in succinct fashion. There are other, briefer interviews throughout the book, many of them snippets of conversations collected as I journeyed by train through New York and Washington, D.C., to Indiana, and finally, from Chicago to San Francisco, in the fall of 1979.

For the most part, the names used in the "Notebooks" are not the real names of the persons interviewed. In the

* See Epilogue, "Middletown, U.S.A."

end, it was felt at least some might have revealed intimate financial information which, for one reason or another, could later prove embarrassing. The exceptions, such as appear in the final three notebooks, were persons who clearly would be classified as public figures.

Aside from those most cooperative and gracious men and women, some of the others who helped me include Chairman Joseph Tamney and the other members of the sociology department at Indiana's Ball State University, as well as Professors Joseph Trimmer and Dwight W. Hoover of the same institution; Ronald Gyure, of Congressman Phil Sharp's office in Washington, D.C.; George Katona, who devised the Index of Consumer Sentiment and was a founder of the University of Michigan's well respected Institute for Social Research, and William Fellner, Sterling Professor of Economics at Yale University and a former member of the Council of Economic Advisers; Thomas J. Donahue, president, Citizen's Choice, Inc., Washington, D.C.; Ernest L. Scott, editor and publisher, San Francisco Book Company; and Judith Ann Yeager, whose patience and critically helpful suggestions are deeply appreciated. Special thanks are due Cynthia Gair, my research associate in Washington, D.C., whose precise and perceptive reports, especially in the areas of federal taxation and spending, provided a highly professional "eye" on happenings in the nation's capital.

R. C. Y.

Oakland, California
June 1980

Notebook 1:

THE OSGROVES

Ken Osgrove makes $30,000 a year but never has any money. The Osgroves have no savings account, eat out just once a month, and then only at fast-food restaurants, and rarely attend films or plays. They try hard to stay healthy. "Getting sick," says Osgrove's attractive, curly-headed wife, Diana, "just isn't in the budget."

The member of a respected accounting firm, Osgrove, a CPA, spends his working hours helping clients manage their money. Increasingly, however, his free time is spent worrying about his own finances. Osgrove fears rates will climb on the loan he needed to buy into his company, that utility bills will go up again as they did last year, that one of the couple's two children will have to see the doctor. Ken Osgrove is frightened: prices are rising faster than at any time he can remember.

"When I started school in 1964," Osgrove is saying in the couple's comfortable living room, "this kind of income seemed simply unbelievable. It was for the rich. I thought if I could ever make that much money, we'd be really sitting pretty. Now I make that much and it's not

1

really all that impressive. With our new house and inflation, the extra income doesn't stretch that far."

The word *stretch* turns up again and again in conversation. "I make $6,000 more than I made last year," says Osgrove, a handsome, prematurely graying man of thirty-three, "but $6,000 doesn't really stretch very far. The groceries and gasoline got so high so quick that the extra income doesn't stretch as far as I thought it was going to. I have nothing in case of a dire emergency. I have enough savings in the bank to pay the interest on the loan and that's about all. I'm at a point where I'm always a little stretched, and I shouldn't be—at least I think I shouldn't be—with the income I make."

The Osgroves moved into their present home about a year ago. At $42,600, the price was low compared to new houses in other parts of the country. Still, payments for the couple's $38,000 mortgage come to $440 a month, including taxes. That's a big jump from the $175 monthly for their previous smaller home, even though the 8¾ per cent interest is a bargain.

Other expenses turned out to be higher than the couple expected. Tax reassessments in Delaware County meant an additional outlay of $1,200 a year. Electricity is up 50 per cent, water and sewage fees are more than planned, and the suburban location of the house means the Osgroves consume more gasoline driving to town. "Of course, even if we didn't use more gas, we'd pay 50 per cent above what we did a year ago," rues Ken.

All told, Osgrove figures that $650–$700 of the roughly $1,500 he clears each month goes for house expenses, not counting maintenance and repairs. Because he is self-employed, Osgrove must pay for his own fringe benefits—monthly fees for medical, disability, and life insurance come to $160. Even after buying a side of beef to

2

hold down food costs, grocery bills stubbornly hover in the $100-a-week range. Of the roughly $300 that remains, $130 goes to pay off the family's 1977 Chevrolet. Osgrove tries to scrounge up $200 a month to cover interest payments on the $19,000 bank loan he took out to buy into his firm's partnership. What is left, and many months there is nothing, goes for clothing and recreation.

"Three years ago I was the member of a country club," says Osgrove. "This year I wasn't because I couldn't scrape up the $300 dues anymore. We joined a family swimming pool club and I'm still paying on a loan because I didn't have the $500 initiation fee. I joined the Y, but I joined the cheapest way I could, paying the minimum dues and passing up on the businessmen's club upstairs." For the Osgroves, dinner out usually means McDonald's and then is limited to "major family events." The couple entertains infrequently and only occasionally takes a vacation.

"We're not destitute and we're not going to starve," says Osgrove. "I don't think inflation has affected us that much in how we actually live. But it has affected our idea of where we think we ought to be and whether we are reaching certain goals. I resent the fact that I can make this kind of money and not have anything. It bothers me no end that we don't live any better than we do. It's because of inflation; we haven't thrown money away. We're probably no better off now than we were five years ago. I make more but it all goes out in the same payments that it always went out in. I don't think I'm worse off, but it does really bother me that I haven't gotten ahead. I really thought that ten years after school I'd be on top of things." Diana shares her husband's disillusionment. "I thought we'd be comfortable enough not to worry if we spent $10 on something," she says, "but we're just not there."

"We live in a neighborhood where a lot of people are pretty well off, or they think they are," Ken continues. "Actually, I think a lot of them are doing what we did for a while. You live in an illusion that you're doing better than you really are. Things are good and going to get better and you can go out and live it up. But if you don't plan ahead, you're in trouble. I've been there. We tended to overuse credit cards. In my situation, if I sign my name, I can get anything on credit. One day we woke up and we were facing $2,000 in credit-card bills."

Diana admits that part of the problem was her own tendency to charge clothes and other items for the Osgrove's two school-age children. "If the kids needed something, I just went out and bought it for them," she says. "With peer pressure, of course, they always want it. I don't know why I did it, because I never had those things." The couple have consolidated their bills and are in the process of slowly paying them off.

Diana, thirty-two, is a nursing student at the local university. She enrolled partly for personal development, but a more important reason was economic. "I worked before, and by the time I bought my clothes, paid for the gas and a babysitter, I didn't make anything. This time I wanted whatever I did to have a practical benefit. I wanted to get into something where the work is there and the pay is good, so that if we need the money I can find a job."

The Osgroves have been married fourteen years. Their living room is comfortably furnished; a vintage upright Zenith radio stands in one corner, a gleaming, three-legged walnut table in another. They have a friendly, if yippy dog, a "cockapoo." By all appearances, the Osgroves are settled, stable Americans. Yet their lives are spent in endless pirouettes around the shadow of crushing personal debt. Ken even has had to scrape and borrow

4

to pay his taxes and Diana's education would be jeopardized without a low-interest federal loan that pays her tuition. ("In my mind, I should not even qualify for that kind of loan at my income level," Ken guiltily admits. "But without it, I'd have a problem sending her to school.") How is it that the Osgroves and so many others like them live so close to the financial edge?

"Government has caused part of it," insists Ken. "They continue to expand by trying to take care of each segment of the population. The only way to do that is to print more money; and the more money you print, the less it is worth. We've gotten to a point where we think if the government's paying for it, that's great, we don't care. I'm beginning to see that this big-spending government is taking things away from me and everybody else. The money they squander and waste is adding to inflation.

"We overspent on the credit cards. It got us in trouble so we had to pull back and say, well, we can't do that anymore. The government has done the same thing for years and they haven't pulled back. We've gotten to a point where we've tried to control the threat of depression so much—unions have added to the problem—that even a slowdown in the economy won't stop inflation. The natural part of the free-enterprise system doesn't seem to work anymore. What I'm afraid is that we'll have what happened in the thirties. They say it could never happen again, but I don't see how we can continue as we are. A lot of people are probably going to be in the bread lines one way or another."

Osgrove got a close-up view of how the government operates when his firm was hired to audit a local federally funded Community Development program. The city had received $5 million to turn a former factory headquarters into an attractive site for the location of new small businesses. As Osgrove tells it, most of the money was squandered, providing permanent jobs for perhaps a dozen people.

"Community-Development spending isn't necessarily a bad idea," Osgrove insists, "but I do think you should be able to get something for the money you spend. The Community-Development kinds of programs create jobs but they're very temporary from what I've seen. They generate paper, but they don't accomplish much in bricks, mortar, or moving earth. The old work programs in the thirties at least left behind something you could see."

Is he still proud to be an American? "I can't imagine living any other way. I still have personal freedom in the way I conduct my life. If I want to criticize the government as I have been doing, I can shoot my mouth off and nobody can say a thing."

Yet there are problems, problems special to the people in the middle, the people without hired champions, without political leverage. The biggest problem is time. Those who would hold power must possess time—for meetings, for personal talk, for gossip and conferences and studies and maneuvering. But working men and women never have time; they are far too busy with their working lives. So others take power. And the layering and relayering of government becomes its own best foil. Says Osgrove: "The more structured government becomes, the less easy it is for the small man to have a say in what happens, to have control over what gets done."

Osgrove has seen first hand how little control the little man has, especially over his personal economic destiny. His bid to own a chunk of the system came in 1978, but there was no way he could earn enough to pay back the $200,000 he would have needed to buy out his former partner. It is a hard money tale coming true in hundreds of American towns, a tale of fathers unable to pass along family farms to their sons and daughters, of hardware stores a hard-working clerk can never own, of small-town newspapers forever out of reach of their reporters and editors.

"The only retirement for most small-business people is the equity in their business," Osgrove explains. "Let's say the son wants to take over from Papa, who wants to retire. The son says, I can pay you so much, and Papa says, yeah, but with inflation my business is worth three times that. And the son finds out he can't pay his father what the business is worth and what he needs to live on. So they go outside; a large firm comes in and buys them out. Papa gets what he needs, but the son doesn't own anything. You've created a bigger company and another employee.

"I think people are asking now, why work so hard, you're not going to get anywhere. Even those who are working are looking at different things in their work. It certainly isn't putting in long hours so someday they can get their own business. They're looking at working shorter hours and getting along because that's all they're going to do anyway. Financially speaking, most of the people I know have actually taken a step backward, particularly in the last twelve or eighteen months. I don't see how the person making $10,000 to $20,000 is ever going to get ahead. The pay increases they get aren't going to ever be enough.

"I've been at what I do for ten years now. I've worked the tax season where you're on the job until midnight and you get up at six and you go until midnight again. The kids hardly recognize you by April 15. I've come to the point where I'm asking myself, what am I doing this for? I'm no better off than I was five years ago, so why am I working so hard? The answer is that I'm still working for that thing in the future, that something I'm going to get or be one of these days. There was a time when I sought it, when I really was ready to go after it, but I'm not working as hard as I used to. It's just been in the past couple of years that I have come to that. I've cut back on the hours I'm willing to put in. I guess I'm beginning to doubt we'll ever make it to easy street."

THE TROUBLED MIDDLE

Who is middle class?

Certainly not the famous motion picture actor, reputedly the highest paid worker in the U.S., who commands $5 million a film plus a percentage of the profits.*

His female colleagues in the Screen Actors Guild probably wouldn't qualify either. They earned an average of $4,908 annually in 1979, too little to satisfy most definitions of middle class.

Judge Charles H. Scruggs III, who earned $43,500 annually presiding over his court in Tampa, Florida, seems closest to being comfortably middle class, but he doesn't *feel* comfortable. "I'm disenchanted with the American

---

* According to the popular press, Steve McQueen demands the guarantee of such a figure before he will even consider a script.

dream," Scruggs told the *Washington Post* after deciding to quit the bench for better paying private practice. "I haven't accomplished that much materially."

Who is middle class?

"The Roper Poll shows Americans think middle income means $20–$40,000 a year. Okay, a third of the country does make that much, but by no means the middle third. Nearly two-thirds of the country makes far less. This is the bracket that the public thinks is low income, but it's where the real middle income lies—down around $16,000 a year."—producer Linda Shen commenting on an October 29, 1978, Public Broadcast System inflation report.

"I've got a son who's twenty-eight years old, married and with kids, the same occupation that I had, a meat cutter, and he owns his own home, he owns a new car, he owns a motorcycle and takes vacations and all this. When I was his age as a meat cutter I couldn't do it."—Nevada resident Don Hedrick, quoted in the *Los Angeles Times*, September 2, 1978.

Who is middle class?

Arthur N. Holcombe wrestled with the question in his 1940 book, *The Middle Class in American Politics.* Using then recent statistics that distributed Americans into ten income groups, Holcombe quickly eliminated the top tenth—those earning the munificent sums of $2,600 a year and up—as well as the bottom 10 per cent, who were paid from zero to $340 annually. At that point Holcombe found himself scratching his head. Should he count the entire remaining 80 per cent or just the two groups in the middle, as it were, of the middle? Or was he better off seeking some kind of intermediate combination? "What is the middle class?" Holcombe asked. "How is the middle class to be defined?"

Who is middle class?

Perhaps we should ask instead, who is not? In a famous February 1940 survey by *Fortune* magazine, 79.2 per cent of the public described themselves as middle class. Today, file clerks earning as little as $8,000 and lawyers making as much as $80,000 think of themselves as middle class, albeit sometimes with upper and lower modifiers.

Some analysts prefer defining the middle class by the color of its shirt collars. White-collar workers and professionals—teachers, accountants, lawyers—are middle class. Shop foremen, heavy-equipment operators, and machinists belong to something called the "working class," an apparent leftover of Victorian England, when members of the upper classes considered physical labor demeaning.

But such classifications often bear little resemblance to the world of real money income, in which skilled blue-collar workers earn substantial wages, sometimes higher than those of white-collar employees. Indeed, a California legislative report found that at least two categories of professionals—attorneys and college professors—had lost relative ground compared to the income gains among blue-collar workers during the 1970s. Another key determinant of the economic distance between white and blue-collars—bigger paychecks attributable to college degrees—has shrunk notably in recent years.

"This is outrageous," the physician said when he saw the bill for his plumber's services. "I'm a doctor and I don't earn this much."

"When I was a doctor," replied the plumber, coolly wiping off a Stillson wrench, "neither did I."

10

Income winds up being perhaps the most reliable way of defining what we mean by middle. That way we can include state college professors and licensed electricians, who may well live in the same neighborhood, drive identical automobiles, and have similar aspirations for their children. For an accurate sketch of middle-income America, we may turn to data published by the U.S. Census Bureau and other government agencies. According to these sources, the broad range of income that defines middle begins in the neighborhood of $15,000–$16,000 and extends to something just over $30,000 a year. At the beginning of the 1980s, the average yearly income of American families headed by a full-time worker was $18,000; of those with incomes above $25,000, two-thirds combined the earning power of two full-time paychecks.*

In the end, however, how much the middle makes is less important than what being in the middle means. Middle Americans make the country work. They are the guts of our giant corporations, the foremen and supervisors and line workers in our factories and assembly plants, the farmers who plow our fields and plant our crops. Middle Americans become our college instructors and cops, our computer programmers and technicians, our salesmen and auto mechanics. Impatient to get ahead, to "make something of themselves," they are the strivers, the ones who power the system from below. Middle Americans start more new businesses and buy more houses, purchase more cars and television sets and hair dryers than any other single economic group on earth.

For much of our recent history, the hard work and dedication of middle Americans seemed to be paying off. The country's output of goods and services reached an all-

* For a fuller discussion of middle incomes, see Appendix.

11

time high. Before-tax wages and salaries more than doubled between 1967 and 1980. Indeed, median incomes—the income level that half the people are above and half below—rose 40 per cent in the brief lustrum after 1975.

Yet today most middle Americans find little reason to celebrate. Inflation and taxes are tearing bigger and bigger chunks from their paychecks. For many, unemployment threatens or has destroyed the security of their jobs. Worst of all, they are getting the nastiest feeling a middle American can know, the feeling of not going anywhere. "It seems like every time you think you've done something to get ahead," an Arizona schoolteacher told the *Los Angeles Times*, "something else comes along."

Rummaging through an old trunk a couple of years ago, columnist Pete Hamill's mother found a June 6, 1941, grocery bill whose prices now seem spun from pure fantasy: five pounds of potatoes, 15 cents; five pounds of sugar, 27 cents; a half pound of bacon, 18 cents; one dozen eggs, 37 cents; six packs of cigarettes, 90 cents; one head lettuce, 10 cents; and so on. The total was $4.97. Hamill decided to update the shopping list at a New York City supermarket. Five pounds of potatoes were $1.49; a head of lettuce, 69 cents; six packs of cigarettes, $4.50. All told the bill for the same eighteen items his mother had purchased a generation before came to $28.66, an increase of 477 per cent. "America was killing me," groaned the writer, "a dollar at a time."

The 1980s began with inflation that was chronic and accelerating. During the opening days of the decade, consumer prices were increasing at an incredible 20 per cent. Federal Reserve Board action slowed the price

12

rise somewhat, but at the high cost of rapidly escalating unemployment. To most Americans, the economy seemed to bounce up and down like an erratic yo-yo; their own financial futures appeared dark and doubtful.

Inflation was everywhere. Among twenty selected countries reviewed by the Worldwatch Institute, a Washington, D.C., research group, not a single nation managed to hold consumer prices below their 1950 levels.* In Britain, the price of an average home rose by more than 25 per cent in the twelve months prior to 1980 and general inflation raged at over 17 per cent. "When I was a little girl, we always had a Sunday joint of beef," the schoolteacher wife of an English auto-service manager told the *Washington Post*. "But we can't always afford one now. I guess we seem middle class because of our house and cars, but I don't feel middle class."

Why should those in the middle feel less than middle? At least until a few years ago, members of the American middle class were riding the crest; they belonged to the most affluent society in history. Between their own success and the workings of the progressive income tax system, wealth gradually was being redistributed from the rich to working people like themselves. Wasn't it? "The popular impression," wrote Gus Tyler in *Scarcity: A Critique of the American Economy*, "was that past inequities were being slowly righted . . . everybody was being reclassified into the middle class—upper, lower, or middle middle."

What really happened was something quite different. Though money incomes grew substantially, the distribu-

* Preliminary Worldwatch estimates, based on figures supplied by the International Monetary Fund, indicate only four countries—Japan, Malaysia, Sweden, and West Germany—managed to reduce their inflation rate in 1979.

tion of wealth—tangible financial assets like real estate, stocks, bonds, and savings accounts—changed very little. By the 1980s, the same wealthiest 5 per cent of the population still held 53 per cent of the nation's assets; their share of national income had dropped less than 2 per cent since 1947. Although a major reduction was being made in the ranks of the nation's poor,* the historic American dream of moving upward from one class into another frequently went unfulfilled. To many middle Americans, the seeming contradiction in their failure to record greater gains in real wealth and status, together with what appeared to be the increasingly comfortable circumstances of those below them, was best explained by their own growing economic burden—not only from inflation and taxes, but from both working together.

Nearly three in ten white Americans harbor a "strong sense that the very poor and the very rich are in an alliance with government officials at their expense," concluded author Donald I. Warren in *The Radical Center*, a Ford Foundation-financed study of middle Americans. Warren's exhaustive survey of attitudes among thousands of middle Americans in 1972 and 1975 portrays an increasingly alienated and cynical group of Middle-American Radicals (MARs), frustrated by their lack of power and the perception of a new order in which, "the rich give in to the poor and the middle pay the bill."

For the most part, MARs' power has centered around traditional ethnic and blue-collar issues like opposition to

---

* In 1947, according to the University of Wisconsin's Institute for Poverty Research, 32 per cent of the nation's population fell below official poverty lines, compared to less than 12 per cent by the late 1970s. This was largely accomplished by growth in what the government called "income transfer" programs, like Social Security and Aid to Families with Dependent Children, which took money from one income class and gave it to another.

14

forced busing. But Warren sees a strong MARs element in recent battles to slap tax and spending limits on state and local governments. MARs attitudes are becoming more popular with white-collar and younger age groups, he adds. Indeed, he wrote, "it is possible for a considerable part of the society to develop a MARs orientation, perhaps within a short time period. It depends to what extent they are all facing a common problem."

On AMTRAK's Metroliner between New York and Washington, D.C., a young businessman folds his newspaper and talks briefly with the passenger beside him. "We thought we could make people middle class just by spending money on them and we were wrong," he says. Among other things, he is angered by a system which encourages unmarried, teenage welfare daughters to become pregnant. "All they look forward to is the day they turn eighteen and can qualify for independent welfare payments and a place of their own," he says. "We spent billions trying to make the middle class bigger and we wound up making it smaller."

One thing is certain: more and more working people are learning the language of economics and inflation. Men in steel mills and auto plants and lumber yards seem suddenly aware of a British socialist and economist, dead for more than three decades, named John Maynard Keynes. Housewives quote the Consumer Price Index and carry pocket calculators in the supermarket. Newspapers and television stations expand their coverage to present more economic news. And in California, on a June night in 1978, a large, elderly man, loose jowled and hulking before an election night crowd, spreads his arms for silence: *"We have a new revolution,"* bellows Howard Jarvis. *"We are telling the government, 'Screw you!'"*

15

In many respects, the middle class is hurt the most by inflation and unemployment, primarily because it has the biggest emotional stake in the economic system. Being middle class in America means believing in somedays, that time after the hard work is done and the rewards come rolling in. High prices and joblessness chop down that belief; they replace dreams of somedays with future uncertainty.

Notebook 2:

THE MAGEES

"It really makes me feel useless, I'll tell ya. Not being able to find a job and havin' her more or less support us. I've tried, I've tried hard, but there just isn't no jobs to get. The most depressin' part is knowin' you can't pay the bills." Raymond Magee has been laid off. After working less than half a year, he has lost his $8.20/hour auto industry job. Magee, twenty-seven, is a big man with a sandy-colored, Zapata-style mustache and thick eyeglasses. He and his wife, Jama, who earns $400 a month as a clerical supervisor at a local bank, have been married less than a year.

Magee sits at a wood-grained Formica table in the kitchen of the couple's mobile home. "I was really thrilled when I got hired in there," he says. "I could see a real future at the plant. They're into everything. When I was there, they won a special certificate for their outstanding work on marine motors and transmissions.

"I was disappointed when I got laid off, I'll tell ya. I figured it would be a steady job and I'd be able to put my thirty years in. The way everything is goin', the biggest

17

thing these days is to have security. I thought here would be my good chance to get some money saved up and get a home. My biggest goal, I wanted children real bad, and I was hopin' she could quit her job and have a little bit of family. But it's no sense bringin' someone into the world if you can't make it yourself. Now I'm in this situation where I don't know what I'm gonna do. I sit and listen to the radio quite a bit and play my guitar. I keep the house picked up pretty good for her; I do my share. But sittin' around all the time, it's just depressing. It's bad, it's bad all around."

Magee is proud of his work record, brief as it was. Starting at $6 an hour, he was quickly promoted to the plant's group 19-1, a higher paying production team where his duties included inspecting synchronizers and testing gears. "I knew when I made the group I was doin' good," Magee says. "The hard work was worth it." Within a short time, however, the deep-seated problems plaguing the auto industry were clear to everyone; Magee knew the plant would soon be laying off.

Jama, meanwhile, had been putting away $37 of Ray's $210 weekly check each payday. "I guess it's because I work in a bank, but I like the idea of having a little something to fall back on. I like seeing mothers bring their children in and open an account, even just a few dollars, for them. That to me is teaching the kids something—they're going to learn you don't get everything handed to you."

A shy young woman, Jama has a habit of averting her eyes when she speaks. Yet her voice is forceful as she discusses the sense of disappointment when Ray lost his job. "It seemed like we had just gotten started. Before Ray was laid off we basically did whatever we wanted. We had the money to go to the show once a week. If we wanted to go out for dinner on Friday night, we had the money to do that and still make all the payments."

"Right now, we're having a really tough time," says Ray. He smokes incessantly and visibly flinches each time the telephone rings. "Our bills are something like $700 a month and she brings home less than $200 every two weeks. There's just no way we can make it.

"I'm definitely at fault for going so deeply into debt. I should have waited until I had more seniority. I figured if we got a few loans, you know, and were paying them off real good, we'd have good credit. You have to have a lot of credit established when you go wantin' a home.

"If I had known things were going to turn out the way they did, I never would have gotten the loans. There were things I wanted her to have, but she's the type of person it wouldn't have mattered; she would have been just as happy without them. I just didn't want to wait. There were really only a few things—I wanted her to have a washer and dryer, and I wanted a color TV. I didn't want to wait and get one thing at a time, which I should have done."

The Magees face an awesome array of bills each month. Even in a trailer, gas and electricity come to $65 during the winter. Payment for the washer-dryer is $23. A finance company holds the note for the couple's vacuum cleaner, another $18, and the stereo and television sets add $20 more. Magee owes the company credit union $4,500 for his truck ("I needed decent transportation and when I got the loan from them I figured it would help secure my job"). As if anything could make matters worse, under state law Magee won't be allowed to draw unemployment until next year.

Jama's father has taken over monthly payments for their trailer, purchased in his name. Jama tries to send each

19

major creditor $10 or $15 a month, but coming up with even that token amount can be difficult. The $152 payment for her car is deducted from the first of her two monthly checks, leaving the Magees just $40 to cover gas and groceries for two weeks.

The biggest problem, however, has been constant pressure from four finance companies. "I've done everything but get on my knees and kiss their feet to get them to help," says Magee. "When we applied for the loans, we had the money every time in a couple of hours, no questions. They handed out the money and now we're begging for help to consolidate the loans and get them straightened out, and they won't have anything to do with it. They want more. I said you ain't getting anything more out of me. One wanted us to get the title out of her dad's name and give them the trailer. Those finance companies wouldn't like nothin' better than this trailer, but this is one turkey they ain't gonna get. I'll never go back to none of them, I'll tell you that much, none of them.

"I've come to the point where I don't care. I mean I still care but then again sometimes I really don't. It seems like we just got started and here we are slapped flat on our face. All I want is for Jama and me to be as happy as possible, because I just don't know what's gonna happen anymore. I more or less live for each day now. I'm not tryin' to plan ahead because I can't.

"I don't know who really to blame for it. Look what goes on with Nixon, then Ford pardons him. If that was me or you, you know where we'd be. Not off buying big apartments in New York. To me this country is falling apart, slowly but surely. Like the killings. It seems nowadays you can kill somebody and get away with it. I have a friend and his wife was sitting in a bar having a casual drink. A guy walked in and shot her four times with a .38.

He went to court and said, 'I'm sorry, that was the wrong woman.' Now he's out. My friend's wife is dead because she was the wrong lady and the guy that shot her is walking around. It's crazy.

"I still feel good about being an American. I'm still free. I just wish somebody would come up with more jobs and ways to keep things going. Right now, the government seems to pass bills they shouldn't, and not to pass bills they should. All I want is to work and live comfortably. I don't want to keep up with the Joneses, or the Smiths, or anybody else. I just want us to be able to pay our bills and have a little left over to do what we want."

Jama has been listening intently. Now she speaks, her soft voice blurring the edges of her words. In a few simple sentences about her childhood, she provides an important insight. "All you can hope for is something better," she says. "You don't work for something worse, nobody does. And that's probably part of the reason we're in this type of economy, because you get so much, you want more. That's the way I was brought up. My parents made so much when we were small, and as they made more on their income, they gave us more.

"You don't work to go down; you work for something better. I don't go to work forty hours a week just to see everything I have go out the window. I want to see more of it.

"Right now, I don't know. There just aren't enough jobs. Something drastic is going to have to happen before things get better. When my parents were my age, my mom didn't work. And now I would say every girl I know my age works. So you've got twice as many people looking for jobs. What will happen? I hate to say a war, but that's usually what gets the United States out of a depression."

Ray is hopeful he will be recalled soon. "When I left that Friday, my foreman said he would ask for me back." Still, others have waited months to return to the payroll and the auto industry is slumping badly. Meantime, there have been moments of tension between the Magees. "I'm the kind of person, I'm not going to just lay down and die for these finance companies. Sometimes I get a twelve-pack of beer—Jama thinks I shouldn't, but when I get depressed I get it anyway. I can't make somebody give me a job. Sometimes I say the heck with this, I'm gonna live today.

"I really don't know what the world is coming to. Everything's getting out of control, gettin' out of everybody's hands, out of reach. What is it gonna take to stop things and get people to realize what's goin on? How can you get people to believe there's a gas shortage when as soon as these companies get their price increase you can buy all you want?"

"Everything's gone up so much," adds Jama. "I would love to have a home. But that's just hopeless, really. With things the way they are, you're lucky if you can get a mortgage. The banks don't have any money to loan and the prices are just so high. But I'd sure rather be living in a home right now than this trailer."

Newsreel:

THE ENDANGERED DREAM

In Chicago's AMTRAK waiting room a young couple sit closely together, scanning the newspaper want-ad section. They plan to move here soon and, like most prospective first-time home purchasers, are stunned by the cost of housing. Still, they remain firmly determined to buy. "I always wanted to own my own home," the young man says. "My parents owned their own place and it's part of my upbringing."

Why is home ownership so central to the view Americans hold of themselves and their way of life? For most of our history, purchase of our own shelter has signaled entry into the middle class. The right to hold property put the nation's early citizens on a common footing with the nobility of Europe. Since nearly all the colonists were farmers, property meant control over one's economic destiny; land created the nation's first entrepreneurs.

Nothing formed the character of early America so much as property. In the Old World, the middle classes began as a small segment of urban society, in America as a broad scattering of independent farmers. From the earliest of times, the ability to move up, primarily through the acquisition of property, was paramount. "From out the host of humble settlers," wrote Thomas J. Wertenbaker in *The Shaping of Colonial Virginia,* "there emerged that body of small planters . . . that formed the real strength of the

colony. The poor laborer, the hunted debtor, the captive rebel, the criminal, had now thrown aside their old characters and become well-to-do and respected citizens. . . ."

Individual property ownership has always held powerful political significance as well. "A general and tolerably equal distribution of landed property is the whole basis of national freedom," wrote Noah Webster in 1787. "When this is lost, power departs, liberty expires, and a commonwealth will inevitably assume some other form." More recently, Walter Lippmann found little as important to democracy as each citizen's right to his or her plot of land or homestead. "The only dependable foundation of personal liberty," he wrote in *The Good Society*, "is the personal economic security of private property."

Lacking the institution of private property, Jamestown, Virginia, the first English settlement in North America, might never have survived. For the first years after its founding in 1607, Jamestown was a struggling, semimilitary trading post. Most work was performed by forced labor; sickness was widespread. Hardscrabble poor and landless, the early colonists toiled for wealthy stockholders in England. Winning the right to hold property gave them a stake in their endeavors and salvaged Britain's rapidly deteriorating experiment in the New World. Captain John Smith described the difference: "When our people were fed out of the common store, and laboured jointly together, glad was he who could slip from his labour, or slumber over his taske, he cared not how; nay, the most honest among them would hardly take so much true paines in a week, as now for themselves they will doe in a day." Matrimony, too, was tied to property; only upon marriage was a settler entitled to a house— bachelors lived in barracks.

America's first settlers seldom found the journey to middle-class status an easy one. The early colonists had to fight for their existence, often spending years in servitude before being granted even a small parcel of land, usually fifty to one hundred acres.

Moreover, political theorists of the day often recognized the existence of only two classes, a wealthy, "natural" aristocracy and a sprawling mass of common poor. Melancton Smith, a middle-class delegate to the New York ratifying convention in 1788, drew the ire of aristocrats like Alexander Hamilton and John Jay when he suggested the Constitution be framed to permit adequate representation by the middle class. An urban lawyer and merchant, Smith was convinced that "the body of every nation consists of this class . . . because the interest of both the rich and the poor are involved in that of the middling class."

For most of the 1800s, the United States remained a nation of small businessmen and farmers. Gradually, however, the composition of the middle class changed. Once again, land played a key role. As farming small plots became less economically feasible, small farmers began selling to large ones. By 1870, 10 per cent of the nation's families held 70 per cent of the property; at the outbreak of revolution, they had owned less than half. An equitable distribution of property, wrote C. Wright Mills in *White Collar*, gave way to the privilege of property.

In the new middle class neither the wage worker nor the salaried employee owned workable land. Perhaps it was this very propertyless equality which so enhanced the importance of the single family home.

"I just couldn't live in an apartment. The first two or three years we were married we lived in an apartment but ever since

World War II, we lived in a house. We've owned homes since then. It seems like that's the American way of life—your home is your castle, regardless of what it is or where it is at. And I've always thought of that as a regular home, not an apartment or condominium. To me, that's like staying in a motel."—Indiana retiree, October 1979.

Ted and Paula Duncan have an antique mahogany dining table surrounded by cheap plastic kitchen chairs, a living room that is bare except for two chairs and a lamp, and a bank credit card bill that makes Ted wince. Travel plans have been scrapped, furniture purchases postponed. Like many other young couples, the Duncans purchased a house they cannot yet afford. "But if we waited until we could afford a house, we'd be renters the rest of our lives," says Ted.—San Francisco Examiner, February 25, 1979.

What has happened to real estate in the last quarter of the twentieth century is dizzying, especially considering that as late as 1948 roughly three-fourths of new homes could be bought for less than $10,000. Actor Anthony Quinn remembers buying a Beverly Hills house for $28,000 in 1938, and feeling guilty about selling it for $34,000 to Greta Garbo five years later. In 1978, Quinn returned to the U.S. after living in Europe. His old homestead was for sale, but the price had risen to $1.5 million. "I couldn't afford it," Quinn says. "I just don't have that kind of money."

How had the housing market become so desperate? For one thing, the wave of environmental concern which swept the nation after the late 1960s often resulted in local laws and policies aimed at limiting new home construction, especially near metropolitan areas. Some experts placed most of the blame for the choking off of housing supplies on a coalition of environmental idealists and suburbanites, who had the time and skill to mount effective "no-growth" lobbying efforts. Developers passed along the costs of endless meetings with regulatory boards and commissions in the form of higher prices, which meant the areas where they built became more expensive. "If growth controls become widespread within a region," concluded a University of California at Davis study, "moderate income families might be severely limited in the choice of communities in which they can afford to live."

Some folks, of course, did just fine. Childless, capable of generating large incomes, a new generation of professional couples seemed unhurt by escalating home prices. Together with other nontraditional living groups, they formed the heart of the so-called "gentrification" movement, perhaps the best hope of refurbishing our cities. But the gentrifiers also slammed a heavy door against future urban home ownership by low- and middle-income families.

As the housing crisis deepened, the residential real estate market became increasingly bizarre. In some urban areas traditional American buyers found themselves competing with foreigners who brought along suitcases stuffed with cash to purchase the homes they wanted. Cramped city apartments were converted into condominiums at six figure prices. In Prince George's County near Washington, D.C., county executive Lawrence Hogan sought to outlaw construction of new homes costing less than $85,000 because, he said, a tax-freeze meant adequate services could no longer be provided for moderate-income home buyers. Manhattan-based Harry Helmsley, reportedly the nation's biggest independent landlord, declared urban middle-income housing was fast becoming extinct. Subsidized housing is for the poor, Helmsley told financial columnist Dan Dorfman. "If you're poor, you can afford it; and if you're rich, you can afford it. But for the guy making $20,000 to $40,000 a year—forget it; he's got a very tough time."

Rising costs of land, materials, financing, and labor contributed to the crunch. Nationally, housing starts fell hundreds of thousands of units short of projected needs. In California, a thirty-member governor's task force concluded there was no way new construction could keep pace with the 193,000 additional residents expected annually through the 1980s. "Affordable homes for the middle- and lower-income groups of California's population are just not being built," said the report. "Home purchases increasingly are limited to the upper ranges of income groups."

In the Golden State, one house in four carried a price tag above $120,000 and prices in some counties were climbing $1,000 a week on the eve of the 1980s. Even falling sales prompted by higher mortgages rates could not stop housing costs from mushrooming. "The failure of prices to moderate in line with the reduced activity is evidence of an emerging housing shortage . . . and of intense inflationary pressure within the economy," said John Seymour, president of the state realtors association.

The problem was by no means limited to California, however. The average home price raced past $60,000 in Baltimore, Dallas, and even traditionally inexpensive Seattle-Tacoma. The Federal Home Loan Bank Board predicted that the national medium home price would reach $125,000 by 1988, based on even a "moderate" 7.5 to 8 per cent inflation rate. If, on the other hand, inflation continued at 10 per cent for the rest of the century, a house that cost $40,000 in 1979—an impossible bargain in most metropolitan areas—would command an incredible $325,611 within twenty years. Already the typical middle-income home buyer was spending a third of his or her income on monthly mortgage payments—nearly double the proportion paid seven years before—reported Data Resources, Inc., a Lexington, Mass.-based research firm.

Most important, as the 1980s began, zooming prices and interest rates had pushed the traditional American dream of buying a new home beyond the reach of most first-time purchasers. The majority of those who did buy homes were in the upper quarter of household-income rankings, according to the Congressional Research Service. "The cost of buying and maintaining a single-family home [is] increasing twice as fast as the average family's ability to handle it," noted a prominent housing executive. "This means only one of four families will be able to buy a house in the future."

Government and academic experts called it the "homeownership affordability" problem, but what it boiled down to was an unprecedented phenomenon: for the first time in the United States property ownership was becoming a closed society. For the most part, entry was barred to those not already belonging to the club or unable to obtain a transfer of wealth from close relatives or friends. That great escalator into the middle class, the single-family home, had not only stalled but was slipping into reverse.

First-time buyers, as a group, suffered substantial declines in housing "affordability" during the 1970s. The housing costs for initial home purchasers rose nearly three times as fast as spending for shelter by re-purchasers and non-movers. Reaping the "reward" of higher price hikes for housing, the re-purchaser could still enjoy the thrill of stepping up to a more costly residence, even if family

29

income hadn't grown faster than inflation. The typical first-time buyer, on the other hand, lost ground no matter how successful he or she had been in bringing home a fatter paycheck.

There were other problems.

In prestigious Marin County, an exclusive, sun-washed suburb of San Francisco, rich Iranians were outbidding the natives for housing. In one city, the *average* home price spiraled to $200,000. Among one real estate agent's clients, a Persian engineer plunked down $250,000 for a four-bedroom swimming pool-equipped home; an importer-exporter paid $400,000 for a residence at an exclusive Marin County address; a physician bought a home costing over $300,000. In each instance, the buyers paid cash, closing in days deals that would take ordinary Americans weeks to finalize. During the winter and spring of 1978–1979, the city manager of one Marin hamlet estimated that as many as 40 per cent of its single-family dwellings were being purchased by well-heeled refugees of the Shah's defunct regime.

The foreign presence was felt in the countryside as well. "My sons and daughters and people wishing to gain entry into agriculture cannot purchase a farm and pay for it due to the inflated land values caused by foreign and nonfarm investors," a California farmer complained before a U.S. Senate subcommittee. Not surprisingly, by the beginning of the 1980s, the rural population was being hounded by the same real estate inflation as their fellow citizens in cities and suburbs. A ranch in Oregon that sold for $700,000 in 1975 went on the market for $1.8 million in 1978; in Wyoming the price of a typical ranch zoomed from $500,000 to $1.5 million.

Citizens in the country, city and suburb were losing their traditional hold on private property. Yet individual property ownership, or at least the chance at it, is a basic part of what it means to be an American. For most of us, since we began working for someone else, property has been something we call "a place of our own," usually a single-family home, but more recently often a condominium or owned apartment. By whatever name, "We need to re-establish that home ownership is a fundamental right for Americans," building executive Bruno Pasquinelli told the *Chicago Sun-Times*. Pasquinelli obviously had reasons of his own for making such a statement, but the point was nonetheless well taken. The continued ability to own property is as crucial to most Americans' ideas of democracy as the Constitution itself.

As this book went to press, a major study of patterns in home buying was released by the United States League of Savings Associations in Washington, D.C. Among its key findings: that first-time home buyers have been hit hardest by the economy. Only 18 per cent—a full 50 per cent drop from 1977—of the nation's home buyers were purchasing their first homes in 1979, said the report, entitled *Homeownership: Coping with Inflation*. Those who did buy their initial homes, concluded league researchers after examining 14,000 mortgage transactions, tended "both to have higher incomes and to have relied more on second incomes" than in previous years.

31

Notebook 3:

THE GRAEBERS

"Look for a round barn and turn left," instructs Karen in her gentle country drawl. The Graebers live well out of town, past a small farming community of narrow bridges and white clapboard houses. When you come upon it, it is exactly as Karen has described, a large barn, looming out of the cornfields, painted white and perfectly round. The Graeber farmhouse is only a few hundred yards beyond, a square building with a wide, comfortable porch. A circular driveway runs past the cow barn and the pig crib and the shed where the Graeber youngsters raise rabbits for 4-H Club shows.

"I guess everything we do here has something to do with inflation," says Charles Graeber, holding open the front door. "We eat our own meat, that helps, of course, and we raise vegetables. If you live in town, there usually isn't room to raise a garden. The rent went up last summer, but I can't complain too much; it's not that bad."

Graeber, thirty-four, is a squarely built man of average height; his rust-colored hair is lightly tinged with gray. He wears a faded red, blue and yellow cotton plaid shirt.

33

The furniture in the Graeber living room is neither new nor old, and of a nondescript style. An eight-track stereo rests on a rolling cart and the family's large color television set stands in the corner.

Charles works in the nearby Chevrolet plant as a $7.31-per-hour furnace operator; Karen earns $8,000 annually in her clerical job for the county. But the Graeber's real commitment is to their farm. The couple's five children have won ribbons with their rabbits, and Charles is counting on success with his livestock, primarily hogs, to make his dream of retiring to a farm of his own come true.

"I like the family farm," says Charles. "It's a great place to live, and to raise your children. Out on a farm, kids don't have the chance to get out and run the streets; they've got chores they have to do. I think people all around are better off; they don't have as much idle time. And I think on a small farm they take better care of their livestock.

"The trouble is, everybody wants to live in the country, but they don't want to own land—they want to own a lot. The developer, say, goes out and buys a hundred-acre farm. He doesn't care if he pays $2,000 or $3,000 an acre for it because he's going to lot it off at $4,000 a lot. Then when the farmer buys land, it's more expensive because he has to compete with the developer. He has a hard time buying farmland for $2,000 an acre and making any profit off of it. So the farmer loses out."

Charles is not bitter, but he sees high prices as a threat to his way of life. "Ten years ago, the farmer was getting $2.50 a bushel for corn, almost exactly the same as today. But you could buy a good tractor for $20,000, not $40,000, and gasoline wasn't on its way to $2 a gallon. So for the farmer to make it, he's had to raise the amount he produces, and to do that he has to farm more land. With inflation, it's going to end up where the big ones are doing most of the farming. There won't be too many little family farms."

A man and his family would need five hundred acres to make full-time farming a feasible proposition, Charles figures. At current prices, that would mean an initial outlay of close to $1 million. "Then he's going to have interest, which is out of sight," Charles adds, "say 12 or 13 per cent on the farm, if he bought it today (late 1979), and 18 per cent on his equipment."

The Graebers do what they can to fight inflation. Charles estimates he has cut the family's $900 annual fuel bill to $300 by installing a new $600 wood-burning furnace in the basement. Still, the energy crunch is felt in other ways. Driving to their jobs and taking the kids to school, playgrounds, and 4-H meetings, the couple puts more than seventy-five miles a day on two cars. Karen's American-made station wagon gets only twelve miles to a gallon. "With a big family, you have to have a big car," says Charles, "but it costs more to make those trips—about twice as much as it used to.

"Inflation is caused by greed on the one hand and waste on the other. Another thing is that everybody wants to make $12 or $15 an hour, but they don't want to pay the price of the products they make. People get top union money, and then they turn around and buy a Toyota. If everybody goes out and buys a Toyota or some other foreign car, the people who work for the auto industry will be out of their jobs. And when they lose their jobs, they don't buy televisions, they don't buy toasters, and they don't buy washing machines. So those people lose their jobs. We're all in it together, but people don't see that.

"Welfare adds to inflation, it's a big giveaway. Just look

35

at your paycheck and see how much they take out for taxes. How much of that goes for welfare?

"I don't think you should abolish welfare, but you sure do need to reform it. They pay all these people to be welfare administrators. If you ask me, not too many of them do anything about it. They're all sitting around on their cans. They don't police it like they should. Instead of giving the people money, go ahead and pay their rent and their utilities, but you don't have to give them money to spend. If they want money to buy beer or pay for other recreation, let them get out and work."

Graeber has decided to check on the pigs. He gulps down a last swallow of coffee and heads through the kitchen door, the screen banging behind him. Outside it is clear and chilly; the fresh air contrasts sharply with the close, overpowering stench of the hogs inside the crib, but the strong odor soon fades. "The American people are going to have to learn to do with what they've got," Charles says, patting a large sow. "They are going to have to learn to use less gas, and the auto industry is going to have to help them.

"Eventually, we'll get things straightened out. But I don't think government control of prices will do it. It's the people that's going to have to do it. If everybody quit thinking so much about the almighty dollar, we'd be better off. But I'm proud of the country. I can't think of any other I'd rather live in. We always have come through our troubles and I believe we still will. The American people don't quit."

VANISHING AFFLUENCE

A cold Manhattan wind tears against the edges of granite at Fifth Avenue and Forty-eighth Street. Sleek young women whisk by, perfume and the clacking sound of their fashionable heels trailing after them. Store windows gleam with the golden buckles of Gucci, with fine leather jackets from the great tanneries of Europe, with jewels and imitations of jewels, and with the brushed steel and fluorescence of Japan's latest electronics. In the window of a bank is a sign:

WHAT ARE YOU WAITING FOR?
THE GET WHAT YOU WANT LOAN
Ask for Details

Shaped in the years after World War II, the new middle class, a class of wage earners and salaried employees, sought success in career achievement within large organizations. Wealth came to be measured less in terms of permanent estates and more in terms of consumption. Affluence—more for the many—originated in the years after 1945, wrote economists George Katona and Burkhard Strumpel in *A New Economic Era:* "In the post-World War II years poverty was not eliminated—although it was greatly reduced—and yet the majority of Americans were affluent in the sense that they were in a position to spend money on many things they wanted, desired, or chose to

37

have, rather than on necessities alone. The acquisition of discretion in spending and saving by masses of people represents the essence of the new era . . ."

From 1945–1950 "Citizens literally itched to spend their money," recalled Joseph C. Goulden in *The Best Years*, "for homes, for cars to replace the 1930s clunkers they nursed through the war, for refrigerators and juicy red steaks and nylons and anything else that caught their eye." They had the money to pay for it. Americans had piled up $140 billion in savings and war bonds. Contrary to today's dismal pattern of personal saving, most of the funds were held by ordinary citizens in under-$5,000 accounts. The early postwar years were a time of rising expectations; the country felt as if it stood on the threshold of great possibilities.

"In the twenty-five years after World War II," Katona and Strumpel wrote, "continuing economic growth and a steady improvement in our standard of living were viewed as our natural destiny. In those years, thousands of people reported to interviewers that their standard of living was better than that of their parents and grandparents, and they expressed confidence that it would continue to improve both for themselves and for their children."

The people wanted more, expected more, and after surviving unparalleled hard times, demanded more. Their government and business leaders, meanwhile, endorsed the Keynesian notion that mild or "bland" inflation could act as a kind of pilot fuel for prosperity. Deficit spending would serve the useful task of reducing unemployment—or so it was believed—and as Keynes himself urged, in good times responsible public officials would see to it that the budget showed a surplus.

The trouble was real-life government didn't work that

way. Programs started by politicians spawned their own constituencies and became almost impossible to shut off. Bureaucrats quickly learned that their status grew in proportion to the number of their subordinates and the size of their budgets. No matter: ever-growing government revenues would pay the bill.

These were the golden years, the time when, for a relatively long historical moment, the American middle class stood first at the fountain of power. While it lasted, this new golden age would glisten with achievement, in science, in international politics, and in something it called "progress." There would be more cars and dishwashers and electric toothbrushes and television sets than anyone would have dreamed possible.

By the late 1960s, the golden age was over. The national mood of confidence slipped away like air hissing from a punctured tire. There would be some progress for minority Americans, and an enormous number of government programs—nearly all failures—would aim at bettering the human condition. But in the decade after the assassination of President Kennedy, the middle class of America would find itself on the wrong side of the most critical issues of its time.

Misled by its leaders and having discarded its old ideals of prudence and moderation, the middle class acquiesced as the nation stumbled headlong into three major errors:

(1) It launched an imprudent war, recklessly adding to the public debt of present and future generations.

(2) It failed to curb its appetite for an opulent, consumption-oriented lifestyle.

(3) It soiled its own working and living habitat, adding enormously to the cost of maintaining the nation's physi-

cal health as well as to the expense of conducting business.

So there could be no mystery about the reason the economy was in such a mess by the 1980s. The culprit was not a sinister outside force; America had brought on her troubles by herself.

• THE VIETNAM WAR   The nation's incredible economic strength in the 1960s meant it could afford a "guns and butter" policy—enjoy sustained domestic prosperity at the same time it fought a major war—or so President Lyndon Johnson insisted. A wiser ruler, Henry VIII of England, concentrated his energies on battles with his wives. "War," Edmund Dudley, one of his ministers, advised, "is a marvelous great consumer of treasures and riches."

Direct costs of the Vietnam conflict totaled $137 billion between 1965 and 1973, the year of the cease-fire. But that covered only the line items. Billions more were lost in civilian goods and services that would never be produced because of the war. Spending for refugee programs and veterans' benefits added a long "tail" to the Vietnam price tag. Indeed, by 1973, the nation had already paid out $5 billion to "Nam" veterans and, over the next half century, could expect to spend $50 billion more, according to Eliot Marshall and Tom Geoghegan writing in *The New Republic*. Few disagreed with the principle of compensating and, if necessary, caring for returning military personnel. Still, it was worth remembering that not until March, 1946, upon the death of the eighty-eight year-old daughter of a soldier at the Battle of New Orleans, did the government pay the last of its veterans' claims from the War of 1812. As of 1980, the state of Virginia was still paying

40

benefits to the surviving widows of two veterans of the Civil War.

Besides its direct and indirect costs, the Vietnam War—like all others before it—created a legacy of inflation. Consumer prices, which had been rising at 1 or 2 per cent before the war, were climbing at 6 per cent annually by 1970. With the exception of a two-year surcharge, taxes had not been raised to cover costs of the conflict. The result: a public debt of $317 billion in 1965, which had grown by less than $4 billion annually since 1950, ballooned by more than 40 per cent over the next eight years.

"I think there's no doubt that the generation of deficits over the period of the last dozen years—you take it back to 1965 and the Vietnam war deficits—lie behind this enormous monetary explosion that we've had which is the root cause of inflation. You get into arguments about demand pull and cost push and all of these things but still when you're all done with it, there's been too much money printed."—author Martin Mayer in comment to television interviewer.

The Vietnam conflict wasn't the only reason the average yearly federal deficit tripled after the mid-1960s. But the war resulted in production of billions of dollars worth of tanks and guns and planes that nobody could buy. About half the public supported the war, according to opinion surveys of the time. In the end, however, few Americans were willing to make the personal financial sacrifice necessary to conduct the conflict on a "pay as you go" basis. Hopes for a balanced budget went into a permanent fade.

● THE CONSUMPTION CRISIS We wanted it now, we wanted it pretty, and we wanted it wrapped in plastic—

fast foods, unbreakable toys, and throwaway bottles. If anything was more important than convenience to the postwar economy, it could only have been the incredible array of chemicals that made convenience possible. Regrettably, most of them wound up being derivatives of an increasingly rare sticky substance.

"Oil, that's what causes so much inflation. Everything is either moved by it, or heated by it, or made out of it, one way or another."—Indiana farmer, September, 1979.

Between 1960 and the spring of 1979, OPEC (Organization of Petroleum-Exporting Countries) oil prices rose 807 per cent. Even as late as 1972, the nation was spending less than $5 billion on imported oil; seven years later the tab was $65 billion. As Andrew Tobias noted in *Esquire*, the U.S. could exchange an area of $2,000-per-acre farmland approximately the size of Iowa to OPEC for one year's consumption of oil at current 1980 prices.

The oil crises of the 1970s changed more than the price we paid for a gallon of gasoline or heating oil. The worrisome issue surrounding oil, and many of the other resources threatened by over-consumption, was not only how expensive they would get but also how their restricted availability made us feel. Armed with the knowledge that we were using three times as much energy per capita as the average European, forewarned that we were consuming more food than any nation on earth, we were overcome with a sense of unaccustomed vulnerability. The Great Store was closing and, yes, we were temporarily out of that item. Good-bye, golden age.

• THE ENVIRONMENTAL CRISIS Insatiable demand pushed the start button on a giant industrial machine.

Before too long, some of our lakes and rivers changed colors; our air became hard to breathe; some of us, maybe all of us, began getting sick.

We couldn't stand going outside. It burned your eyes, there was pain when you'd inhale—it stunk, like somebody had died outside your door.

I know the fear in the pit of your stomach when you think about getting cancer. There is a definite risk of cancer here.

—resident and government scientist discussing contaminated chemical dump at Love Canal, New York. *San Francisco Sunday Examiner-Chronicle*, August 13, 1978.

The ecological impact of human industrial activity, and how the nation reacted to it, is easily the most complex of the major historical developments underlying the great inflation of the 1970s and 1980s.

At the same time industry pushed hard against the frontiers of petrochemistry and other technologies to satisfy our appetite for consumer goods, environmental pollution was having a damaging effect on human health that, in turn, increased medical costs. Industry argued that the expense of scrubbers, settling ponds, and other pollution-control equipment amounted to billions of dollars a year—spending that usually was passed along to consumers in higher prices. A study for the Council on Environmental Quality, however, insisted that only 0.3 to 0.4 per cent of the average inflation rate after 1970 could be attributed to federal environmental regulations.

Both arguments ignored the impact of environmental damage on spiraling medical costs. Cancer now afflicts more than 25 per cent of all citizens during their lifetimes and causes the deaths of one in five. "The consensus is growing in the scientific community that most human cancers are environmental in origin, and thus ultimately preventable," wrote Dr. Samuel S. Epstein, in the March 1977, *Bulletin of the Atomic Scientists.*

As Dr. Epstein notes, industry groups have branded legislative efforts to control many carcinogens as inflationary. Yet the continued contribution of cancer to rising health costs draws little notice. The direct and indirect annual costs of cancer, responsible for millions of hours of lost earnings and productivity, not to mention 365,000 lives each year, was estimated at over $18 billion by the U.S. Department of Health, Education, and Welfare.

"In June of 1978, I was ordered to cut back on the regulations, to soften them to make them easier on industry because of the President's fight on inflation."—William Sanjour, government physicist formerly in charge of drafting rules for the disposal of hazardous waste.—*Chicago Tribune,* October 7, 1979.

Business had a point: inflationary dangers did exist in unreasonable application of environmental regulations. But an alternative of higher medical bills seemed a poor trade-off, even from a purely economic standpoint. If nothing else, the environmental crisis made us keenly aware of how complicated our lives had become. There were no simple answers in a world of limits.

"The thing is, everybody's interrelated, depending on everybody else," said the Indiana farmer. "I used to think, well, if things got real bad at least we've got our own milk. But now I think differently. If things get bad enough, I suppose the people will come out to the farms. They'll come out and eat corn on the cob, if there's any corn out there. They'll be eating cats and dogs, I reckon. I don't know. That may be way down the road and it may not."

BOB AND AL

"Your work is your identity," Bob says. "If you don't have a job, you're nothin' in this goddamned country." Bob is the local union head at an auto battery plant. A twenty-five-year veteran of the assembly line, he has curly brown hair and a face that looks like wadded pink paper. Now, in a hotel lobby, he is talking about how his members feel about working, the government, and inflation.

"We're just factory hands," he says, his voice low. "But we want to make things better for our children, see to it they have more education, so they can have a better shot in life than we did. The trouble is, every time you turn around, tuition and board is up at the colleges and universities. It used to be a guy could hire on at a plant, save a few dollars, and then start a business or buy a little farm and get out. That's all over now. Everything is franchised, so the little guy is more or less stuck where he is.

"In the beginning, GM and all the big firms said automation was going to be a boon to mankind because

45

we could produce so much that costs would be down where everyone could afford the products. It hasn't worked: our batteries are higher now than they ever have been and we have less men. When I was shop chairman six years ago, we had 1,300 to 1,400 people counting those on sick leave. There were so many lead burners on the line, you could hardly get elbow room. Now that they're automated, we're down to 568 workers."

Across town, Al is talking about some of the same issues, though from a different perspective. Al is an important executive at a large corporation and, at thirty-seven, earns $24,000 a year. Keenly intelligent, politically conservative, he places most of the blame for inflation on wrong-headed government policies.

"My idea of the American way," says Al, "is that it should leave people free to advance themselves. I have been working very hard, getting a job and working my way up, so I deserve to keep what I earn. The system would be appropriate if it would allow me and everyone else to do that. To a certain extent it does not, because of inflation and the high level of taxes. I resent it. Since 1972, my salary has doubled, but I think in terms of buying power; it's about the same. Maybe we're slightly ahead, but not very much."

Echoes Bob: "I'm smart enough to know inflation and unemployment are the enemies of democracy. The reason is that working people finally get discouraged. They lose confidence in their leaders. We keep saying to our representatives, 'Cut costs a little, try to save.'

"We elect these people, then they go up to Washington and it seems as if they represent themselves. Our congressmen should get off their asses and try to think things out instead of simply throwing money here and there and everywhere. I couldn't believe we shipped kerosene to the

Arabs when their refining facilities broke down. Our people read this in the paper and they say, 'What the hell is going on in Washington?'

"The men are disheartened. They feel the government is not trying to help them with the real problems they've got. Government means well, but something happens. You enact a law and all of a sudden you've got a monster that consumes you. Our people are patriotic, they believe in the system. But they aren't sure how to get it working again. Their dilemma is this: how the hell do you stop the government from wasting a lot of money?"

Al believes inflation acts like an acid on the country's sense of confidence and national self-respect. "People feel cheated," he says. "The system right now is punishing people for doing things that are basically a virtue. Being productive, the more you earn, the more the government takes. The more you save, the worse off you are because of inflation. On the other hand, if you don't work, you are rewarded by welfare. That begins to get to people. 'Why should I work?' they ask. "Why shouldn't I cheat a little bit here or there?'

"Things are very different today," concludes Bob. "Before, when we talked about it, inflation was just another big word. The workers on the line, they know now. They feel it all the time. It used to be they'd write their congressional representatives about the gun law. Now they're writing about their concerns over the economy. Our people are more aware of inflation now than at any time in history, or at least any history I know about."

Newsreel:

THE NEW INFLATION

"Tonight we're going to try to look behind the headlines at the most maddening, infuriating problem that's touching everyone of us. Inflation. Like the weather, everyone is talking about it, nobody seems to know quite what to do about it. What we do know is prices are going up for just about everything we buy. Wages are going up too, but never enough it seems."—public television commentator Marilyn Berger in a May 3, 1979, report on the economy.

"We probably have the same gripes as any family in the country. Our electric bill averages $45–60 a month, our gas bill runs as high as $80 a month in the winter. The cost of food—we go to the store and spend $100 and don't have much to show for it. It wouldn't be so bad if prices went up once a year, but it seems like they go up every couple of months."—midwest auto worker, September 1979.

"We worry about the effects of radioactivity on the environment. We are militant about industrial pollution of the air and water. But what about the degradation of the financial and economic environment—the value of money—by inflation?"—J. A. Livingston, *Oakland Tribune*, September 1, 1978.

48

If inflation continues its spiral, today's economic science fiction will come true in the twenty-first century:

• Assuming wages are held to a 5.75 per cent yearly increase, the average worker will be making $656,000 annually within 70 years.

• Assuming price hikes are held to 10 per cent, a Big Mac hamburger will cost $6.51 by the year 2000.

• Assuming tuition, room and board increase at 15 per cent a year, the cost of a four-year undergraduate program at a top private university will exceed $100,000 by the turn of the present century.

Even before the 1980s, inflation was hitting us hard. A shelf survey in one California county between February 1978, and February 1979, showed notebook paper (two hundred sheets) increasing from $1.25 to $1.98; fabric (per yard) from $2.35 to $2.85; Valium (one hundred 10 mg tablets) from $22 to $30; and greeting cards from 35 to 60 cents. Nationally, it was much the same story: cereal and bakery goods up 11.4 per cent for the year; hotel and motel rooms, 13.1 per cent; shoes, 8.7 per cent. Between February 1979, and February 1980, real spendable earnings in private industry fell 7.3 per cent, the largest drop since the Labor Department started collecting monthly statistics on workers' buying power in 1964.

Even being a youngster was getting expensive, as reported in a December 21, 1977, edition of public television's *MacNeil-Lehrer Report*. In "The Cost of Being a Kid," executive editor Robert MacNeil described the financial battering of the younger generation by inflation. In the five years since 1972 bubble gum price had climbed

220 per cent; lollipops were 100 per cent higher; chocolate bars had jumped 162 per cent per ounce. One little boy, a New York City elementary student, summarized his own experience. "Once I saved up for about two months for this thing I got," he said. "It used to cost $5, but then it got raised to $7.50. And I had to save for about two more months to get it."

The advertising industry discarded its reliable catchword "inexpensive" for a new term, more suited to a time of chronic inflation—everything from shoes to sealing wax became "affordable." But economists had a grim term of their own to describe what was happening. They said the price rise could be characterized by a phenomenon known as "the ratchet effect." And they warned that if the ratchet kept cranking, nothing was going to be cheap or inexpensive, or "affordable" even, much longer.

"The ratchet effect" amounts to another way of saying that inflation will not go away, even in bad times. After every recession since the 1950s, the base rate, or floor, of consumer prices has moved steadily higher. Viewed this way, current increases are part of an inflationary continuum dating back to World War II.

In its classic form, inflation is a relatively simple monetary ailment—too much money, usually paper money, chasing too few goods. Imagine a primitive society whose members use red beads as a means of payment. As long as the number of red beads in circulation remains constant relative to the supply of items members of the society wish to purchase, the value of each individual bead stays about the same. If, however, the number of beads increases without a corresponding increase in the things people wish to buy, the value of each bead can only decline. It is a law as old as time.

50

In the United States, the number of red beads in circulation is sharply affected by actions of the federal government. Only the government can make more money available, whether the stimulus for rising prices appears to come from excessive demand—too many people armed with cheap dollars—or from costs pushing prices up, as it were, from below.

The most common way the government overloads the system is by spending more than it takes in. To cover its expenses, the government sells interest-paying securities, in effect IOUs drawn on the taxpayer. Initially, these securities soak up private-sector dollars that would otherwise be used to build factories and homes. This constriction of funds drives interest rates up and soon the Federal Reserve begins printing new money—to buy the securities back and return interest to its lower rates. Recently interest rates deliberately were allowed to remain high in a desperate attempt—widely denounced by prospective home buyers and others seeking credit—to clamp down on growth in the money supply.

There is nothing new about "printing press" inflation, usually synonymous with paper money unbacked by metal. "Not worth a Continental" was more than an abstract slogan during the American Revolution. In December 1776, $1 in coin equaled $1.50 in bills issued by the rebelling colonies' Continental Congress. A year and two months later, the ratio was $1 to $6.84; and by April, 1781, $1 in coin was worth $146.67 in Continental paper. George Washington fretted over inflation's effect on the war effort. Recruitment became increasingly difficult, desertions frequent, the forcible seizure of supplies from farmers unwilling to accept paper money more common. "Can we carry on the war much longer?" the general asked in a letter. "Certainly no, unless some measure can be devised, and speedily, to restore the credit of our currency."

America would experience inflation later in its history, of course. During the Civil War, gold and silver virtually disappeared from circulation as the government struggled to meet its obligations with wildly fluctuating "greenbacks." During the steep price rise following World War I, milk increased by more than 50 per cent a quart and fares on New York City streetcars doubled. Still, the feeling persists that the inflation of the 1980s is somehow different and more difficult than those of the past.

To begin with, it *is* the worst inflation in memory. Only during the last six months of 1951, when prices rose at an annual rate of 14 per cent, had inflation blazed so nearly out of control. But there are other differences as well, some of them at least as troublesome:

• *The new inflation comes at a time when the supplies of many raw materials are being exhausted.* As author Paul R. Ehrlich suggests in *The End of Affluence*, industrial nations such as the United States are rushing headlong toward a petroleum nightmare in which, by century's end, their demands for energy may exceed total world production. Oil, however, is just one item that has become scarce. Availability of lumber and other building materials, other fossil fuels, cereals, metals, and animal protein is becoming limited. In a report entitled "Inflation: The Rising Cost of Living on a Small Planet," Robert Fuller of The Worldwatch Institute cited these examples:

(1) Firewood, principal source of fuel for one-third of mankind, is in short supply. In parts of India, gathering enough wood to heat an average household for one week takes the gatherer two days.

52

(2) Increasing scarcity of easily accessible domestic oil has forced the Soviet Union to step up by five times its exploration and drilling activities in Siberia, where adverse climate and geography doubles the cost of oil.

(3) There have been huge investments in the world's fishing fleet during the past decade, but the global catch remains essentially unchanged. Per dollar spent, the catch has fallen considerably.

In *A Guide to Post-Keynesian Economics*, British economist Joan Robinson contends that growth in supplies of feedstock materials can no longer match industrial expansion. Meanwhile, higher material and energy costs add to the cost of living and prompt cries for wage and salary increases. The cycle of inflation becomes a closed circle.

• *The new inflation is concentrated in the necessities.* In the 1920s and 1930s, the cost of a new Duesenberg, among the finest luxury cars of its day, could easily reach $20,000; Chevrolets and Plymouths and Fords could be had for under $1,000. Today, luxury cars can still be purchased for $20,000 or thereabouts, but auto transportation for the masses has become a $6,000 to $10,000 extravagance.

The point is that today's increasing prices have affected life's basics more than life's extras. From 1970 to 1977, reports the National Center for Economic Alternatives, a liberal research group, the cost of medical care shot up 68 per cent, while the price of power boats, custom jewelry, and champagne rose by only 41 per cent. During 1979, necessities—energy, food, housing, and health care— leapt by 17 per cent, well above the 13.3 per cent increase in the general Consumer Price Index for all goods, according to NCEA's figures. Since four of five families spend two-thirds of their budgets on necessities, the ability of high interest rates alone to curb inflation seems increasingly doubtful.

• *The new inflation appears to refute many widely held assumptions about the economy.* Chief among these is the belief that inflation and full employment are somehow permanently linked. The idea that high prices mean more jobs and, presumably, social progress, gave inflation and, by implication, deficit spending, a respectability in the years following World War II. In the 1970s, the formula went haywire. Despite a persistently overheated economy, unemployment remained stubbornly high; and instead of wiping out deficits, prosperity was accompanied by a spiraling national debt.

Much of daily financial life seems to make little sense. Wages in some labor and public-employee unions rise at the same time unemployment in those very groups climbs. Major American corporations, headed by presumably able business executives, totter on the edge of bankruptcy and run to Congress for help. Economists call what has happened "stagflation"—the combination of slow growth, unemployment, and rising prices—but they are at a loss to explain it. What has gone wrong?

An intriguing answer was suggested in a 1978 Columbia University Ph.D. thesis by Byung Yoo Hong, an industrial and managerial engineering student. Essentially, Hong proposed that large industrial companies no longer sought, as they historically had, to minimize costs to attain the greatest profits. Instead, they maintained desired rates of return by following the path of least resistance—they simply passed higher costs along to the consumer.

Citing industry figures, Hong argued that increasingly high machinery costs had discouraged many firms from

54

investing in new equipment—the American stock of metal-working machinery, for example, is the oldest of any industrial nation. The lack of new labor-saving technology led to an unprecedented decline in output among production workers. From a position of world leadership between 1947 and 1964, annual productivity growth sank to 1.65 per cent between 1965 and 1975, lowest for any industrial nation.* Funds that might have fostered private sector innovation—and, presumably, increased productivity—were instead invested in military hardware and weapons research. Concluded Hong: "The reduced opportunity for a productive livelihood for Americans along with institutionalized inflation have this society facing the modern-day dilemma of high unemployment and high inflation simultaneously."

• *The new inflation seems beyond the control of either citizens or their government.* With much of consumer inflation concentrated in the necessities, there often appears to be little the average person can do to curb rising prices. Similarly, the government finds itself facing a steady escalation in costs it cannot curtail—approved spending on previously legislated programs, for example, and interest payments, usually around 10 per cent a year, on the nation's burgeoning $820 billion debt. Five-eighths of all federal expenditures are affected by mandated upward adjustments to offset inflation, according to the Congressional Budget Office. Programs like Social Security and federal employee retirement pay—which are directly tied to the cost-of-living index—represent more than a quarter of total government outlays. Thus, a 1

* The 1.58 per cent productivity rate increase from 1970 to 1975 was only half that of the economically distressed United Kingdom.

per cent increase in inflation causes about a 0.6 per cent hike in total federal spending—automatically.

At least as disturbing, however, is the rapid growth in so-called Eurodollars, "stateless," unregulated dollars held overseas. For all practical purposes, Eurodollars did not even exist two decades ago; today hundreds of billions in uncontrolled Eurodollars whirl through world markets, growing with every jump in the price of oil. Meantime, foreign investors have used the cheaper Eurodollars to finance acquisitions of U.S. manufacturing firms, real estate, and banks, helping to drive up U.S. inflation in the process. The success of Federal Reserve Board action in 1979 and 1980 to stem the Eurodollar invasion remains to be seen.

• *The new inflation has become self-perpetuating.* In past eras, even as recently as the early 1970s, Americans initially reacted to inflation by increasing savings in an effort to halt the slide in their financial assets. In the "good old years," such action helped dry up excess consumer spending. The current inflation, however, has made fools of the solid, solvent Americans who stuck by cash-on-the-barrelhead and money in the bank. By the end of the 1970s individual and corporate thrift had reached a thirty-year low; the U.S. had the lowest rate of personal savings in the industrial world.

Being frugal had become a dumb idea. The double whammy of taxes and low interest rates hit savings so hard that people with straight passbook accounts actually lost money. Those who put their funds in the stock market did little better. During 1973, a good year for the market, investors reported taxable gains of $4.6 billion. But when prices of the shares were adjusted for inflation, the $4.6

billion gain turned out to be a $1 billion loss. "It is little wonder," said *Business Week*, "that consumers, expecting a chronically high inflation rate, are putting their dollars into tangible assets rather than financial assets." In fact, rules were liberalized in 1979 making higher interest rates available to the average citizen, but even with these changes the anti-savings bias of the federal tax code—which treats interest as straight income—wiped out any real gain for most savers.

The discrediting of individual financial prudence has been accompanied by what economists call an "inflationary ideology." Not only do business firms resort to "anticipatory pricing" to cover expected cost increases, consumers grow anxious to buy now, regardless of the price. Why wait? they ask. The prices of everying we want can only go higher. The expectation of continuously increasing costs thus becomes a self-fulfilling prophesy.

There have been attempts to explain away the pain of inflation for ordinary Americans. Some observers, among them government officials anxious to minimize the ravages of recent inflation, point out that income and residential property values have been zooming up right along with prices. "Over the last ten years," insisted Peter McGrath in an October 1978 article in *The Washingtonian*, "the middle class not only has kept ahead of inflation, but also has improved its position." Such arguments, however, suffer from one or more of the following flaws:

(1) They attribute higher than realistic incomes to the middle class. McGrath, for example, includes persons in the $40,000 salary range as middle class, an income level actually enjoyed by approximately 5 per cent of all families.

57

(2) They ignore the desperately low rate of savings, and the extremely high credit exposure even among those in upper-income brackets.

(3) They treat the increased value of homeownership as if it were an easily transferable gain in actual worth, comparable to bank savings. This unfortunate misconception will become increasingly difficult to defend if high mortgage rates continue. Homes constitute a highly illiquid asset whose increase in value ordinarily may only be realized when a family decides to purchase another home, at an equally inflated price.

(4) They consistently overlook the mounting financial obstacles facing those wishing to gain entry to the middle class through such traditional activities as purchasing a house or an automobile or acquiring a college education.

(5) They do not acknowledge that a steady erosion in the sense of financial well-being is directly attributable to reduced growth in real income. Inflation grinds down our perceptions of everyday life.

"It's not easy out there if you wonder where the next refrigerator payment is coming from, or if your kids are going to eat, or if they're going to close down the plant where you work. There's not a lot of security out there."—singer-songwriter Tom T. Hall, *Washington Post*, December 5, 1979.

"I feel good about my own future, but I worry about the young people growing up. You think, if the inflation keeps going, what they'll be paying for a home. Our kids all have homes but we have eight grandchildren and we just wonder how they'll ever own a home."—senior citizen, Ann Arbor, Michigan, October 1979.

Notebook 5:

HURLEY, JACKSON, AND JENNY

The word *welfare* makes Hurley C. Goodall wince. One of five black representatives in his state's legislature, Goodall today is a respected leader with a secure position in the community. As a child, however, his father died when he was three and the family was forced to go on relief.

"My mother was getting $30 a month to raise three boys, and one of my brothers had polio," Goodall, now in his fifties, recalls. "She went out one time and did voter precinct polling and made $30. She did it to buy shoes for us, because we didn't have any shoes to wear. Anyhow, somebody told the welfare office and they took the $30 away from her. I saw my mother sit down and cry. She'd been out in the snow and rain and ice trying to buy us shoes for school. And I swore to myself, as long as I live I never want to be on a system like that. I remember that and I couldn't have been over seven or eight years old. It made me hate the welfare system worse than anything."

"I lived on welfare all my life and I don't have anything against it," says Jackson Tragg. "My mother had to do it and I think in some ways it made me a stronger man. But now I think more people have to depend upon themselves; they have to get away from asking the government for help."

Jackson Tragg is twenty-seven, black, a $10,600-a-year Comprehensive Employment and Training Act construction inspector. A handsome young man with an athletic build and a trim Afro haircut, Tragg was active in high school and college sports; at the same time he was an early supporter of racially balanced cheerleading squads and the creation of campus black studies programs. Perhaps because of his concern for the less fortunate, Tragg is increasingly dismayed by the present welfare system.

"They've encouraged people to be lazy, both black and white," he says. "The federal government attitude has been that if these people don't get a job, or nobody hands them a job, they should still be able to live off of the government. I say the real answer is give these people jobs. But if they don't want to work, take them off the aid."

"When I went to welfare to see about getting help, they told me my daughter and I should be able to live on $147 a month. That's rent, utilities, groceries, clothing, everything. I told the man at welfare the only thing I knew to do was to get a gun and shoot me and my daughter and then nobody will have to worry about us."

Jenny Roswell is white, a large woman with a wide smile and an intelligent, deliberate way of speaking. Jagged cracks skid down the walls of her small home, but the floors are clean, and the worn, sagging furniture has been freshly mended.

"My husband is an alcoholic and we're separated," she continues. "It embarrassed me to death to go up there and apply for welfare. And it embarrassed me to go to the bank and cash a welfare check. I just didn't want to be classed with welfare. Or on food stamps. Other than my parents helping me out, I've never had to depend on anybody but myself. I've heard people talking about welfare cases. People always put welfare people down. I have too. 'Look at her,' they say. 'What's wrong with her? She can go out and get a job doing something.' Well, you can't when there are no jobs to be had."

"Some people do need welfare, don't get me wrong," protests Jackson Tragg. "There might not be jobs in their area. That is the key problem: we're not expanding the job opportunities. But I'm talking about areas where there are jobs. The caseworkers know what's going on. If they would go into the homes and get these people to work, it would eliminate a lot of the problem.

"Let's take a woman named Mrs. Pearl. Say she's gettin' $220 a month for AFDC, but say they can get her a job making $400 under the Work Incentives (WIN) program. If Mrs. Pearl doesn't want the $400 a month, and to work to get what she wants, then I say the government ought to put a stop to it and make it clear she doesn't have any justification for being in the program.

"People have been pacified with that $220 a month—if they know they're going to get that, they're satisfied. It shouldn't be that way. If a person can get a job, they should get off their butts and get to work."

At the time of her separation, Jenny was receiving $348 a month in CETA funds while she attended accounting, bookkeeping, and office machines courses at a local business college. Graduating with an "A" average, she approached the job market with high hopes. "Every place I went, they said, 'Do you have experience?' I typed seventy-four words a minute and I still couldn't find a job; I couldn't even get work in a motel making beds."

After spending two months on welfare, Jenny finally landed a CETA-funded job. But she only clears $228 every two weeks. Out of her first check each month comes $100 for rent, $33 for the payment on her 1971 Buick, $11 on a deep freeze, $25 for sewage, $16 for gas, $6 for water, and $20 "I'll have to pay back to somebody because I had to borrow $20 to make it to payday. I thought I was getting ahead, just getting a job, but I found out I'm not getting ahead at all."

"It's getting outrageous," Jackson agrees. "The only life I see is that you work and pay to stay in debt. Every time you turn around, something is unexpected. It frightens me. I know that my pay isn't going that much higher. Sometimes I think, 'What am I going to do?' My head just drops and I say, 'Damn!' I'm sure other minorities are in the same boat, though maybe they are too macho to say it. I'm not."

Two years ago Jackson and his wife Sharon moved into an inexpensive home in the black community. Sharon earns about $7,000 in a clerical job with a local advertising agency, and Jackson recently started his own small business, a cocktail lounge, to bring in some extra cash. Even so, money is tight. "Right now it's pretty hard just to meet the basic bills, the house payment, and utilities," Jackson says.

"I can't go into the store and buy what I would like to buy," observes Jenny. "A lot of times, I have to tell Michelle, we can't get something because we can't afford it. It's kind of bad to have to tell a kid you can't afford it, something other kids have. It makes me feel like a dummy, it really does. Other people's kids go to the bowling alley, they go skating on Saturday and Sunday afternoons, they go to the movies. Michelle asks, 'Why can't I go?' And I really don't have any answers. Except that I don't have the money.''

Under law, Jenny's CETA job will end after eighteen months. "The thing I hope is that somebody will notice that I want to work and do well," she says. "I want to do a good job; I don't want to feel I'm just going in and taking the money. I like to feel that I have put in a good day's work when I come home. I think everybody does."

Hurley believes an overhaul of welfare would make it easier for people like Jenny, who really do want to work, and harder on freeloaders. But he cautions against expecting too much from welfare reform. "I don't think it's fair to blame welfare for all our problems," he says. "I think sometimes people are looking for a scapegoat. When I get upset and angry, I fall into the same trap.

"I resent paying for it just like other people do. I start saying, 'All those welfare people have Cadillacs and they're too lazy to go to work.' And I do see some young girls around with two or three babies waiting for a check every month, but they aren't in the majority.

"I would feel much more comfortable with a system that helped old people all they needed, but where some of these young people would have to go to work or starve. You could take one mother on a block and pay her good wages to take care of the other mothers' children. That would enable the others to go to work and take care of themselves and their families. It would help break the welfare cycle.

"The present system cripples people. It is cruel and unusual punishment against the people it is perpetrated upon. They sit there and wait for somebody to do something for them and they never do anything for themselves. We sure aren't helping these people."

THE DOUBLE RIP-OFF

"Even though politicians today can see that these welfare programs are horribly destructive to the economy, to individuals, to their ability to survive, they still will not challenge them. Because to do so, they'd have to challenge the moral base. They'd have to say, look, it isn't right to take money forcibly from those who earn it and give it to those who don't. No one in politics today will say that."—corporate executive discussing inflation, October 7, 1979.

"I've always heard the rich get richer. I guess that's the way it really is. The rich don't care about anybody else; the more they get, the more they want. That's the whole thing: more money. It seems like if you've got money, or you know somebody who's got money, you're all right. The rich people don't care; they've got things fixed up pretty much so they can't lose."—auto industry worker discussing inflation, October 15, 1979.

Middle Americans feel squeezed on both sides by the present economic system. Zooming state, local, and federal taxes have hurt middle-income families most, adding 90.6 per cent to their combined tax burden over the past twenty years, twice the increase for upper-income groups, according to a recent study.* Yet the vast majority of families that earn $15,000 to $30,000 a year receive neither the numerous social-welfare benefits provided for the poor, nor the income-boosting tax loopholes available to higher-income citizens. "We are up against the wall and going nowhere," wrote John C. Raines of middle Americans in *Illusions of Success*.

While the factory worker totes a lunchbucket his wife has stretched the family budget to fill, armies of upper-bracket corporate types are writing off their noonday meals as "business expense." Welfare recipients are packing their youngsters off to school without any lunch at all, secure in the knowledge that the kiddies will get a warm meal free—paid for by the government.

Housing is another sore point. While climbing interest rates, prices, and down-payment requirements have virtually frozen middle-class buyers out of the market, government-subsidized housing for lower-income Americans has expanded by billions of dollars a year. Indeed, some private builders have been forced to adopt "inclusionary" policies, setting aside portions of their developments to be sold at cost to less-advantaged purchasers—whose new neighbors are left to pay the bill through higher home prices. Meanwhile, of course, upper-income citizens are writing off bigger chunks than ever of their mortgage payments, thanks to the workings of the progressive income tax system.

* "Significant Features of Fiscal Federalism," May 1979, Advisory Commission on Intergovernmental Relations, Washington, D.C.

Can middle Americans be blamed if, from where they stand, it increasingly appears as if two welfare systems exist, and they aren't benefiting much from either?

Consider the disturbing evidence, piled up in the fine print of repeated government studies, that some welfare recipients are better off than the working taxpayers who pay for their benefits. "Especially when medical care and food benefits are added to cash, a female-headed family on AFDC can fare better than families headed by workingmen and workingwomen never eligible for AFDC," concluded an exhaustive welfare study by Congress in the early 1970s. Contrasting actual case histories, the report compared household "A," a low-income working husband with a wife and two children, and household "B," a welfare mother with three offspring. After computing the cash equivalent of food stamps, health care, AFDC, and other assistance, congressional researchers concluded that the so-called disadvantaged welfare family, household "B," actually came out ahead, by $343 a month.

"National welfare programs," concluded a 1978 study by the Washington, D.C.-based Heritage Foundation, a conservative research group, "are essentially earnings-redistribution programs in which the earned incomes of some workers are taxed to provide unearned incomes, in cash and in kind, to other workers and nonworkers." The combined annual growth of the federal welfare system was averaging 25.11 per cent, three times faster than the annual growth in wages, reported Charles D. Hobbs, the study's author.

As the 1980s dawned, the situation seemed little changed. A single-parent, low-income family with two children theoretically would be eligible for twenty-three national welfare programs including Medicaid, food stamps, free nutritional supplements for mothers and infants, free school and summer meals for school-age children, low-rent housing, free child care, family planning, legal assistance, and job training, according to Hobbs. A hypothetical welfare mother with four children living in Portland, Oregon, could enjoy an equivalent, untaxed income of $13,799, according to 1969 estimates by the Congressional Research Service. A decade later, Hobbs calculated that this figure could top $20,000 annually, given inflation-adjusted growth in welfare plus expanded benefits.

"The system is becoming lax, that's what's happening," says a young black. "Food stamps, for example, are a waste. They need to go back to the old system where they gave out cheese, eggs, milk, chopped beef, and Spam and made sure the people were eating properly. The trouble with the program now is that when people who have been poor get food stamps, they're going to buy steak when what they need is four pounds of hamburger. Give them the food so they have to eat it; otherwise it's just more wasteful spending."

"I have nothing against legitimate welfare but the fact is people are abusing these things," says a union man. "I think most of the food stamp people are not working people, but voting people. They'll vote for whoever will promise them more. My wife and I went to the store recently and the gal ahead of us bought about $150 worth of groceries, including nice, thick cuts of meat. We can't afford to buy those things. I told my wife: 'She'll buy those with food stamps,' and she did. She had two shopping carts full of groceries and took them out and put them in a car that was newer than ours."

If the present tax system redistributes middle America's income into nonproductive welfare programs, the same tax system encourages nonproductive investments by upper-income citizens in activities deliberately designed to lose money. And that is just one questionable impact of the tax "breaks" or "loopholes" available to those in higher brackets. Since 1974, such dodges have been labeled "tax expenditures" in official budgetary language, recognizing their equivalency, in terms of spending, to free abortions and atom-powered tanks. By whatever name, for at least a decade tax evading gimmicks have been multiplying faster than the number of wealthy widows in a stockbroker's telephone book.

Legally deductible expenditures by businessmen, ostensibly hard at work between sips of Chivas Regal and nibbles of *crêpes flambées*, have drawn some of the sharpest criticism. "A lot of lavish living is being subsidized by average taxpayers," Robert M. Brandon, director of the Ralph Nader-affiliated Public Citizen's Tax Reform Research Group, told the House Ways and Means Committee. A New York City businessman successfully billed taxpayers for 338 $20-plus lunches in a single year, Brandon reported, citing Treasury Department records. Another man, an electrical-fixtures sales representative, wrote off breakfast, lunch, and dinner—five days a week. In all, top executives averaged $30,000 a year in expense-account benefits. "If that $30,000 were salary," testified Brandon, "they would have to pay taxes on it, just as the rest of us have to pay taxes before we entertain ourselves."

The system creates infuriating inequities. In 1977, for example, Rockwell International, a defense industry giant, paid no U.S. income taxes despite profits of well over $100 million. The company bragged in a *Fortune* article that expense-account spending by its twenty-four top executives had not exceeded $500,000 that year. Just 12 months earlier, however, Senator William Proxmire criticized Rockwell for entertaining, at taxpayers' expense, nearly a hundred military and government brass at company hunting facilities and retreats in Chesapeake Bay and the British West Indies. Other firms have leased salmon streams in Iceland and villas on the coast of Spain for corporate—read taxpaid—entertaining, according to Brandon's group.

Businessmen almost instinctively defend such expenditures as essential to commerce and hence inherently productive. But even the pro-business *Fortune* article found it hard to give that idea unqualified endorsement. "When corporate jets descend like locusts on the Super Bowl or Masters," wrote Roy Rowan in the magazine's April 24, 1978, edition, "it would take a brave defender of business indeed to argue that the income produced by the outing will exceed the sums expended."

But if the link between high-flying business junkets and actual, productive work seems disturbingly vague, what about welfare programs that discourage even passing involvement with the world of paycheck toil? Government studies have repeatedly concluded that the welfare system is having a negative effect on national productivity. The combination of slashed benefits and higher taxes if a welfare recipient accepts employment sharply reduces the attraction of work, especially the low paying variety usually available.

Can it be surprising that many heads of low-income households are reluctant to seek employment? "When disposable income (after taxes and work expenses) plus benefits available at various income levels are considered," reported a study of welfare by the Joint Economic Committee of Congress in 1973, "it is clear that in relation to the basic social programs including medical care there is no advantage . . . in increased earnings." A 1979 report in *Challenge* magazine was more specific. Thanks to the

69

combination of higher taxes and reduced benefits, said its authors*, the average AFDC (Aid to Families with Dependent Children) benefit reduction was 40 per cent.

In other words, for every dollar of earned income, benefits are reduced by approximately 40 cents. Because AFDC beneficiaries also receive Food Stamps, with their 30 per cent [reduction] rate and often reside in public housing where rent subsidies decrease as earnings increase, their cumulative tax rate is nearly 70 per cent. Furthermore, the Medicaid notch, which completely terminates a recipient's eligibility as soon as income reaches a certain level, pushes the tax rate over 100 per cent . . . those groups who offer less labor in response to high tax rates—the aged, disabled, female heads, the unemployed, married women, and the poor—confront higher combined marginal tax rates than anyone else in the economy.

Welfare spending directly fuels inflation. It reduces work incentives, leads to overspending by government, and offers benefits that weaken consumer resistance to higher prices. Food stamps are one example of the latter phenomenon; government-paid medical care is another. Since Medicare and Medicaid were enacted, the federal share of personal health costs has tripled from 9 to 28 per cent. "Beneficiaries were encouraged to demand more and better services, while providers were free to incur higher costs without a worry that patients would either resist or be unable to pay," reported a recent major study for the Joint Economic Committee of Congress.† The result? A seemingly unstoppable rise in health costs.

* Danziger, Sheldon, Garfinkel, Irwin and Haveman, Robert, "Poverty, Welfare, and Earnings: A New Approach," *Challenge*, September-October, 1979. All three authors are associated with the University of Wisconsin's Institute for Research on Poverty.
† *Income Transfer Programs in the United States: An Analysis of Their Structure and Impacts*, Sheldon Danziger, Robert Haveman, and Robert Plotnick, all of the

Widespread inequities exist in the distribution of welfare. Low-income recipients in some states get several times as much in benefits as they would in other states. The system directly encourages marital instability by awarding higher benefits to fatherless families. In Michigan, for example, families earning the minimum wage can increase their incomes by a third if the father leaves and the mother goes on welfare. In twenty-five states and Puerto Rico, a family with no earnings becomes eligible for AFDC *only* if the father deserts. Combining public assistance, food stamps, school lunches and Medicaid, an "intact" (i.e., father-headed) welfare family of four receives 26 per cent less in benefits than a female-headed family of four.

It would be one thing if the government's efforts to reduce poverty were working. But liberals and conservatives agree they are not. Between 1965 and 1974, spending on job training for disadvantaged workers grew from $30 billion to $170 billion. Yet the conclusion of the Joint Economic Committee/University of Wisconsin report is that only through direct income assistance such as AFDC and food stamps—in other words, direct cash or cash equivalent payouts—has any progress been made against poverty. The idea of giving the poor a "hand up" to earn their way out of poverty has failed: "If only earned income is considered," said the report, "the aggregate incidence of poverty has remained unchanged."

In contrast, from the standpoint of the middle-American pocketbook, the tax write-off ripoff has worked all too well. Business meals and entertainment deductions are

previously cited government-financed Institute for Research on Poverty, University of Wisconsin, Madison. Part of the JEC's Special Studies on Economic Change series, the report was completed in May 1979, but had not been released by mid-1980.

running between $12 billion and $15 billion annually, accounting for nearly one dollar in four at the nation's eating and drinking establishments, according to estimates cited by government economist Steven D. Braithwait in the February 22, 1979, *Congressional Record.* The unanswered question, of course, was how much deductible martinis, Welsh rarebit, and steak tartare had added to the price of dining out for ordinary, non-expense account Americans. The Revenue Act of 1978 clamped down on some entertainment expenses, but protected the deductibility of theater and sporting event tickets, country club dues and fees, and most wining and dining expenses.

No-one knows how much income upper-bracket taxpayers keep because of tax loopholes. But Stanley S. Surrey, a former Harvard law professor and assistant Treasury secretary for tax policy, believes individual benefits could be enormous. "If the actual data were made known to the public," he wrote in a *New York Times Magazine* article, "the result would be a national scandal that would surely produce serious tax reform." Surrey continued: "Every informed tax lawyer knows of individuals with very high incomes whose actual tax payments are on the same level as those of restaurant employees or mechanics or others who service their affluent lifestyle."

Robert W. Whitaker, the conservative author of *A Plague on Both Your Houses,* believes wealthy Americans have benefited as much from the welfare system as they have from tax favoritism. Financed largely by middle-income taxpayers, vastly expanded social spending programs helped the rich stave off rebellion among the poor and preserve their own wealth and status. Moreover, claims Whitaker, a new priesthood of public employees is committed to aiding the bottom rung of society and prepared "to defend the interests of that group, expressed almost invariably in terms of greater health, education and welfare expenditures, against those of the middle class."

American society is therefore generally and increasingly split into a coalition of rich and poor against the middle. Like almost all social organizations, there are numerous exceptions. The liberal, new-establishment, education-welfare coalition comprises the upper-middle and lower classes. Their enemy is not the rich, but the working class, the lower-middle and middle classes.

Whitaker's portrayal of deep and permanent fissures in American society may be overdrawn, but it nonetheless illustrates the way many ordinary citizens increasingly view their economy. Following are some of the income-increasing laws, loopholes, programs, and other benefits available to those at the upper and lower ends of the income spectrum but mostly denied those in the middle.

A. POORFARE

"We in America today are nearer to the final triumph over poverty than ever before in the history of any land." Herbert Hoover's confident 1928 campaign proclamation foundered on the rocks of the Great Depression, but the nation has been striving toward that elusive goal ever since. Such efforts peaked nearly forty years later, when Lyndon Johnson, promising Americans "man's first chance to build a Great Society," declared war on poverty. Johnson's battle cry filled many with hope, but it also signaled a new wave of government spending.

RICHFARE/POORFARE: *How Much Income Assistance Programs Cost Average Taxpayers* Each Year*

Data developed from proposed U.S. Budget, Fiscal Year 1981–82

Major Assistance Programs for Low-Income Americans			Major Assistance Programs for Upper-Income Americans		
Program Description	Program Total**	Cost Per Capita	Program Description	Program Total**	Cost Per Capita
Cash Assistance	$ 20.0	$ 157	Capital Gains Tax Breaks	$ 23.4	$ 184
Food Assistance	14.7	116	State/Local Tax Breaks	24.7	195
Fuel Bill Assistance	2.4	18	Investment Write-Offs	16.9	133
Health Assistance	62.4	492	Charity Deductions	9.8	77
Direct Housing Assistance	10.1	79	Income Security Exclusion***	129.9	1,026
Employment Training and Placement Assistance	11.8	93	Home Mortgage Interest	22.3	176
Education Assistance	14.9	117	Reduced Rates, Corporate Income	7.5	59
Legal Assistance	.33	2	State/Local Bond Exclusion	9.3	73
Community Development, etc.	7.0	55	Consumer Credit—Itemized Deductions	48.7	384
			"Business" (wining and dining) Expense	15.0	118
Totals	$143.63	$1,129	Totals	$307.50	$2,425

Total "Richfare/Poorfare" Tab: $3,554 per capita

* Per capita figures are based on Census Bureau estimates of 126.6 million taxpayers in the U.S. in 1976, the latest year for which such figures are available.

** in billions of dollars

*** Includes social security, unemployment compensation, and other government assistance payments, as well as private company and self-employed retirement programs.

Indeed, increased state, federal, and local outlays from 1955 to 1975 "can be attributed almost entirely to the growth in income-assistance spending," concluded a 1977 report by the nonpartisan Congressional Budget Office; with continued expansion, welfare expenditures could equal one-third of GNP by century's end. Increasingly, such spending does not even show up in welfare checks— "in-kind" services like medical aid and food stamps now far outdistance cash payments to the needy.

The explosive growth of welfare spending began with the Johnson Administration programs of the 1960s. For example, food stamps were launched in 1964, partly to help support farm prices; by 1980, the program was costing $8.7 billion annually, a growth of 20 per cent in just four years. Federal spending for Medicaid, approved by Congress in 1966, reached almost $14 billion in 1980, a 50 per cent jump from 1976. About half of 1980's multi-billion housing programs were enacted in the 1960s; by the late seventies, housing assistance outlays were rising at 20 per cent a year; such spending is expected to grow by $1 billion a year through 1984.

"There were many sources of the increase in costs," concluded the Joint Economic Committee study.* "They included, among other things, increased leniency on the part of welfare administrators, expanded rights and entitlements stemming from the initiatives of organized groups of recipients and legal rights activists, more liberal court interpretations," and other factors, including "a reduction in the stigma attached to being on welfare."

Twice as many welfare programs were enacted during the 1960s—a time of prosperity—as came into being in the 1930s, a time of unrivaled depression. Social welfare

* *Income Transfer Programs in the United States*, ibid, p. 17.

accounted for more than one-third of the $600-plus billion proposed budget in 1981. The executive department that runs most welfare programs—the new Department of Health and Human Services (HHS)—is the Cabinet's number one spender, even though it no longer manages education, as its predecessor agency, HEW (Health, Education and Welfare), did.* Here is a brief guide to the low-income welfare programs Americans, mostly middle class Americans, pay for:

• CASH ASSISTANCE Aid to Families with Dependent Children (AFDC) is designed to meet the "necessary costs of living" for single-parent families and, in twenty-five states, families headed by underemployed fathers. Supplemental Security Income (SSI) payments go to the low-income aged, blind, and disabled. In mid-1980, AFDC payments were being increased and expanded to cover 300,000 new recipients and SSI payments boosted to reflect a 13 per cent cost-of-living adjustment. Together, AFDC and SSI represent some $14.3 billion in the 1981 budget. (The SSI program has been rocked by recent allegations that monthly payments in excess of $300 routinely have been doled out to convicted murderers and other felons classified as "disabled.") The "Earned Income Tax Credit," a reverse income tax designed to provide incentives for low-income wage earners, doubled between 1979 and 1980, becoming a $1.5 billion program with six million recipients; further growth is expected through 1982. Counting state programs, the total taxpayer outlay for cash assistance to low-income citizens will soon be well over $20 billion.

* The $222.9 billion budget of HHS is followed by the Defense Department's $158.7 billion. One cynic calculated that the $228 million earned during a recent year by Du Pont, one of the nation's largest corporations, would keep HHS running for less than half a day.

• FOOD ASSISTANCE Besides the Agriculture Department's food stamp program, fifteen separate federal food programs assist states in feeding low-income and other needy persons. These include school lunch, school breakfast, summer food, child care, and elderly feeding programs, expected to add $4.2 billion to the nation's publicly assisted food bill during budget year 1981. Another $860 million for the supplemental food program for Women, Infants and Children (WIC), represents a doubling of expenditures in a single year. Abuses under the food stamp program were significant enough to require 1977 rules tightening eligibility for students and specifically banning the stamps for households owning luxury cars.

• FUEL ASSISTANCE In late 1979, President Carter signed a $1.5 billion bill designed to help needy Americans pay their soaring home fuel bills. Under the measure, SSI recipients received between $34 and $250, depending on weather conditions in their geographic areas; separate funds were distributed by individual states, usually to AFDC or food stamp recipients. A significant expansion of this spending category should be anticipated in the future.

• HEALTH ASSISTANCE Medicare and Medicaid are expected to cost $60 billion in 1981; outlays for Medicaid alone, which pays nearly all health and medical costs for low-income recipients, make it welfare's costliest effort. Meanwhile, benefits are being extended to hundreds of thousands of new recipients as health care costs skyrocket. Indeed, the Medicare Trust fund will be bankrupt by 1992 unless hospital costs are controlled or new financing is found, according to federal experts. Meanwhile, other free or inexpensive health services for low-income persons include maternal and child health services, family planning, home health services, and the National Health Services Corps, as well as community mental health, drug abuse, and alcoholism programs. Under the proposed Child Health Assurance Program, an additional two million low-income children and 100,000 low-income pregnant women would receive medical aid.

• HOUSING ASSISTANCE Some of the major housing programs for low-income Americans: Lower Income Housing Assistance, Public Low-Rent Housing and Home-ownership, Rural Housing Assistance, and special aid for government-subsidized housing projects in financial trouble. Several efforts funded under the amorphous Community Development program include housing components, such as rehabilitation loans and the Neighborhood Reinvestment Corporation, both aimed at stimulating revitalization of inner city neighborhoods. Costs of federally assisted housing programs are expected to top $34 billion in 1980. Mismanagement is widespread in the programs, and the Housing and Urban Development Department has conceded its efforts at reform have not succeeded; the General Accounting Office reports HUD has been forced to take over more than two thousand housing projects in financial difficulty.

• EMPLOYMENT TRAINING AND ASSISTANCE They go by a variety of names—Comprehensive Employment and Training Act (CETA), Youth Employment and Demonstration Projects Act, Work Incentives (WIN) program, Community Service for Older Americans, Unemployment Compensation—but altogether in 1981 they will represent an $11.9 billion effort by working taxpayers to help chronically or temporarily unemployed fellow citizens

78

land a permanent job. Training and "related" programs, scattered through more than a half-dozen government departments and agencies, add another $3.5 billion to the bill.

• LEGAL AND EDUCATIONAL ASSISTANCE Low-income legal assistance, funded by the government's Legal Services Corporation, was a $71 million program in 1975. Five years later it had quadrupled, and for 1981, outlays are projected at $329 million. Educational assistance for low-income students is provided primarily through the Elementary and Secondary Education Act, and 1981 expenditures are estimated at $3.9 billion. Financial assistance for higher education has provided aid for needy college students since 1965. As college tuition costs escalated, benefits have been expanded to include students from moderate and middle-income families; an $815 million program in 1971, it had grown to $4.7 billion by 1980. Estimated 1981 outlays are $5 billion.

• COMMUNITY DEVELOPMENT, COMMUNITY SERVICES, HUMAN DEVELOPMENT The fast-growing Community Development program is an $8.8 billion giant that includes funds for everything from disaster relief to helping state and local governments cope with the impact of drilling activities on their coasts. Its primary aim, however, is improving inner-city conditions. The program is closely tied to "urban initiative" efforts such as the Liveable Cities and Neighborhood Self-help programs. A proposed $200 million National Development Bank would stimulate private investment in areas with high unemployment and slow growth. Even the dry language of the U.S. budget concedes that "a precise accounting of the amount of federal resources currently allocated to urban areas is

79

difficult," but a conservative guess would be that Community Development funding specifically earmarked for low-income assistance is at least $5 billion. Spending for "human development" programs, such as Head Start and vocational and adult-education programs, is estimated at $1.7 billion for 1980; Head Start spending will rise 74 per cent in the four years between 1977 and 1981. The Community Services Administration, which includes VISTA volunteers and other programs aimed at the disadvantaged, gets around $500 million.

B. RICHFARE

"We have to pay taxes but they should be fairer. Plain working people, clerks like me, get paid the very least and taxed the very most. We don't have a chance."

"Taxes should be simpler and fairer. No deductions for anyone. Everybody should pay the same. There would be plenty of money for roads and schools and necessities if everybody paid taxes."
—respondents to query "What is your main objection to taxes?" in *San Francisco Chronicle* "Question Man" column, April 15, 1980.

Tax loopholes—as measured in dollars of "expenditures"—used by upper income Americans have increased some 186 per cent since 1971, according to the Public Citizen's Tax Reform Research Group. Fiscal 1980's $169 billion in tax expenditures—about one-fourth of overall federal spending—is expected to rise by 59 per cent to $269 billion in 1984. Following is a brief tour of some of the favorite ways those who are better off become more so:

• CAPITAL GAINS Touted as a means of stimulating investment and hence employment, capital gains tax expenditures have jumped 42 per cent since 1978. Under the law, 60 per cent of the profits from the sale of securities, real estate, and other investments held for longer than six months may be excluded from taxable income.

Those with earnings above $100,000 receive more than half of all capital gains benefits; indeed, only one taxpayer in ten receives any benefit at all. The average capital gains benefit to a middle-income family was $19.06 in one recent survey year; the average benefit to a family earning over $100,000 was $19,431. Capital gains transferred at death or by gift are not taxed at all.

• DEDUCTIBILITY OF STATE AND LOCAL NON-BUSINESS TAXES The biggest benefits of this break go to those in the $50,000 and-up class, whose per capita benefits in 1980 are estimated at $12,130. This exemption has been used to justify bigger non-federal spending programs, since state and local governments can impose higher levies than the populace would tolerate if it did not exist.

• INVESTMENT TAX CREDIT Primary beneficiaries of this huge write-off are corporations, though individuals will get some $3.2 billion in 1980 tax breaks as well. Critics say the credit has encouraged purchase of machinery that is not economically justifiable, offers little benefit to new businesses that have not made a profit (because it offsets taxes), and generally fails to increase investment in equipment enough to justify its cost, up 14 per cent since 1978. A report by the General Accounting Office found that spending for new plant and equipment generally would have taken place with or without such devices as the investment tax credit; since the credit was authorized in 1962, gross private investment as a percentage of the Gross National Product has not changed appreciably. Meanwhile, the credit will cost taxpayers $15.9 billion in 1980, with 70 per cent of the benefits going to the largest one-tenth of 1 per cent of the nation's businesses.

● EXCLUSION OF INCOME SECURITY PAYMENTS Money from social security, welfare, disability insurance, workmen's compensation, some unemployment insurance, and veterans' disability payments is not taxed. Company pension contributions and earnings are excluded under a formula that allows the employer to deduct payments into a pension plan while the employee excludes the transferred amount from taxable income. Thereafter, income received by the plan from managed investments is tax-free. When the employee withdraws the pension income, it is taxed at reduced rates.

Despite an obvious inequity in this loophole—people who receive social security and other forms of public assistance are taxed at a lower rate than those with the same amount of income from other sources—most of us would agree with the general notion of at least partially shielding older and less fortunate Americans from taxation. But we all know what happens to good intentions and this tax break seems to be no exception. Because big pensions go with high salaries, 49 per cent of its benefits—the largest of any single category—go to those with incomes above $30,000.

● HOME MORTGAGE INTEREST Many analysts have identified this break, which eliminates any federal tax on income used to pay home mortgage interest, as the one which is of clear benefit to middle Americans. However, because of the progressive tax system, wealthy taxpayers benefit far more. A taxpayer in the 22 per cent bracket, earning, for example, $22,000 per year, saves $22 for every $100 of mortgage interest deducted from taxable income. For those in the 70 per cent bracket (someone earning, say, $200,000 annually), each extra $100 of mortgage interest will bring a $70 savings. In other words, the more the wealthy taxpayer spends on mortgage interest, the more he saves. There are no limits on the amount of mortgage interest deductible, so families that own more than one home can mount up large deductions.

• DEDUCTIBILITY OF CHARITABLE GIFTS   All income donated to charities is tax-free, but higher-income taxpayers get a bigger subsidy for their generosity than those in lower brackets. The reason is the same "progressive" tax mechanism that affects mortgage interest. For example, a cash gift of $100 by someone in the 70 per cent tax bracket costs the individual $30 and the government—or, more precisely, other, lower-income taxpayers—$70. A taxpayer in the 25 per cent bracket, on the other hand, would pay $75 of the same gift himself. When property is donated, the government loses both the amount of personal income tax and the capital gains tax not received (contributions of capital assets which have increased in value are deducted at the appreciated value, without being taxed on that increase). Thus, the government often loses more in uncollected taxes than the total worth of a gift.

• REDUCED RATES, FIRST $100,000 IN CORPORATE INCOME   The first $100,000 of taxable corporate income is taxed progressively at rates from 17 to 40 per cent. Income above $100,000 is taxed at 46 per cent. Designed to help small businesses, the graduated rate on the first $100,000 has the side effect of providing tax shelters for high-income taxpayers. By incorporating, the owner (or stockholders) of a small business can shelter up to $50,000 at a 20 per cent tax rate, up to $75,000 at a 30 per cent rate.

• EXCLUSION OF INTEREST ON STATE/LOCAL DEBT   State and local governments sell bonds to build toll bridges, sports stadiums, and convention centers. Interest is exempt from federal taxes, providing an important source of tax-free income for corporations, commercial banks, and wealthy individuals. Eighty-five per cent of the benefits from this break go to those with incomes above $50,000 annually.

• DEDUCTIBILITY OF INTEREST ON CONSUMER CREDIT   Interest on auto loans and other consumer purchases, as well as carrying charges, may be deducted from taxable income. Unfortunately, those most burdened by credit buying—low-income and lower middle-income families—typically receive no benefits because they use the standard deduction. Thus, more than one-third of the benefits from this tax break go to those earning above $30,000 a year.

• LIMITED PARTNERSHIPS   This is fast becoming the upper-income American's ultimate weapon against Uncle Sam, providing the full advantages of a tax write-off at the same time it limits the liability of individual partners in case the project fails.

Imagine, as the Congressional Budget Office did, the purchase of a hypothetical $1 million apartment complex, in which outside investors come up with a $140,000 down payment. As a limited partner, an investor who provided 10 per cent of the equity ($14,000) may legally add 10 per cent of the $860,000 in borrowed money to the base used to compute his or her depreciation, interest, and property levy deductions for personal taxable income. If such deductions come to $270,000 over five years, our limited partner can deduct $27,000 of that amount, nearly twice the original investment. In practice, the total return will be even higher: when the partner "cashes out"—i.e., when the project is resold, presumably for a higher price—the proceeds will be taxed at the lower capital gains rate. A typical limited partnership is deliberately operated to "lose" money during its early years, then sold at a profit.

While discussing advantages provided to upper-income Americans through the tax system, it might be well to reconsider their stake in low-income assistance programs as well. As sociologist Theodore Caplow notes:*

Physicians receive much larger payments from the Medicaid program than their indigent patients receive from any of the programs that offer assistance to the poor. Landlords receive much larger dollar payments from HUD's rent-subsidy program for low-income families than those families obtain from all the assistance programs combined. . . . The fees of legal aid lawyers greatly exceed the wages of their clients.

The net effect of the system, argues Caplow, is to "subsidize persons at every income level more or less in proportion to their non-subsidy income." Even under "Poorfare," it would seem, the rich get richer.

---

* See Epilogue: Muncie, Indiana, "Middletown, U.S.A.

Notebook 6:

THE McCOLLS

"I've got twelve years' teaching experience, a Ph.D. from Stanford; a number of my articles have been published and I've written a book. I won a prestigious national fellowship. I make $16,500 a year." Steve McColl is thirty-six, an intense man with a dark beard and curly hair. At the moment, he and his wife, Betty, are recalling an unhappy experience—the denial of Steve's tenure at the major eastern university where he had been teaching.

"He got caught in the squeeze when they were still supposedly hiring people for tenured jobs even though they couldn't keep them," Betty is saying. "They couldn't be honest about it, so they squeezed you out without any good reason. We both felt the injustice of the system because he had excellent qualifications and the students loved him. He worked hard at the university. We felt our own economic future was imperiled because the teaching market was closing down, so no matter what your qualifications were, there was no guarantee you could get work."

Steve picks up the story. "Every year the classics—my field—has a national convention which is for the sharing of intellectual gains made during the year. The convention also serves as a meat market where people who are buying come to buy and those being sold come to be sold. I went on the market in 1976, the year the meeting was held in New York City. There were 350 applicants and thirty-five positions. Of the thirty-five, less than half were permanent positions, which meant they were bringing you in with no guarantee of tenure. There was enormous tension and tightness at that meeting."

Steve already had made a preliminary exploration of alternate career fields and, confident he could find a job outside the teaching field, attended the convention in a cocky mood, despite the odds. "I'd ask questions like how many of your folks are now tenured; how many are coming up for tenure review in the next five years; and what's your tenure quota? With most of them, it became very clear that unless you put out three books in five years, your chances of a permanent slot were about as good as a snowball in hell."

Steve's wariness stemmed from the fresh memory of his tenure rejection by university administrators who disregarded a positive faculty recommendation. "They are able to keep turning over faculty like myself. They can knock me out—I was making $14,500—then hire somebody up for $11,000, keep them for five or six years, turn them over, and then pick up the next one. It's a crummy situation."

In better times, Steve's outstanding academic credentials would have insured him a position with a more prestigious university. But he chose his current employer—a state university with a solid if not glittering reputation—because it offered security. There are five McColl mouths besides his own to feed.

"We never had a dream that we'd live in such and such a house or have a certain kind of furniture," says Betty, a thoughtful woman with rosy cheeks, sparkling blue eyes, and rust-colored hair. "We were mostly interested in just being together; life was going to be great. And so many good things did happen. We went to Europe for a year. And even though we lived on very little money, it was fun, it was like the child in you could just keep going on and on. We had a baby at the time but that didn't matter.

"The year he lost the job was a very bad year; the possibilities of a job in the future seemed very poor. We could have sat around feeling depressed, and we did for a while, but then we just decided to go away for the summer. So we got out an old tent and camped for two months. We piled everybody in the car and went back to California. It didn't cost a lot of money except for gas.

"Most people would have gone crazy. There was no air conditioning, the car was cramped, and when we went through Phoenix it was 105 degrees. But everybody kept their spirits up. Even children, when their expectations are not great, can be very accommodating. They can sleep on the ground and take it as it comes."

Despite the McColl aversion to materialism, they can't ignore the hard reality of tight economic conditions, admits Betty. "You start out as a youthful idealist, thinking money isn't important and we'll just live hand to mouth. I don't think people who go into teaching expect to make a lot of money, but when salaries don't keep up with the cost of living, you can see why faculty unions keep getting more support. We feel we're living comparably to how we did at Stanford on a $5,000 graduate stipend twelve years ago, because that was tax free. To me, that's the major impact of inflation, when I think about how we lived twelve years ago and how far our finances stretched back then."

"My original financial goal was to make $15,000 a year," says Steve. "The figure $15,000 was $5,000 more than my folks were making at that time and I figured if I had 50 per cent more than that, I'd be okay. Now I think I have a good deal less buying power than they had at that time, and they had five kids. Even at $30,000, we wouldn't be on easy street. If the car conked out, as it's going to do next year, it would still mean we would have to cut back in an area that we couldn't cut back in.

"Inflation—if you allow yourself to become frustrated and anxious about it, it could eat away at what living is supposed to be all about. You can't save any money, so you can't really live for the future; you live just month to month. And when we say we're dry at the end of the month, we're DRY. It's gone.

"January, February, March—for some reason the first three months of the year are always horrendous. Things get tense at the end of each of those months. By then, we're in debt to Sears or Penney's for Christmas spending and things we buy in the fall when we're still a little flush. When the money gets tight, that puts pressure on the love relationships and we sometimes start snapping at each other. 'Why can't I have that record? Why can't I do this, why can't I do that?' No matter how right-hearted everyone is in trying to be nonmaterialistic, that's how things are, because that's the culture we live in."

Sometimes, Steve admits, the pressure makes him wonder about his commitment to the classroom, which on good days is so strong he'd be willing to teach for nothing. The temptation, he says, is to move into administration, where the money is better. "But it's a whole different life," Steve quickly adds. "It's much more like the corporate model where you have to say a lot of yeses and do a lot of smiling.

"When we took that camping trip, I stopped off at Stanford and went in to get my graduate file updated. The guy in personnel counseling said, 'Listen, with your grades, why don't you come back here, do two years in the MBA program, and I'll guarantee you twenty-five thou coming out?' I said, 'I know that, but then I'd have to pay my dues.' And he said that was true, I would.

"It would mean leading a style of life radically different from that of a teacher. If you're a company man, you have to bust your hump. You run out of time you can call your own. You have to say you're really interested in the money and what you think is power at that level. To do it the right way, you move on up and become assistant to the right person.

"To set that kind of goal and invest that kind of time means you're closing a number of human potential doors. People close those doors in quest of economic affluence and are told—it's reinforced—that if you work hard and keep moving, you'll make it, you'll get the kind of money you want, to buy the kind of things you want. You'll feel secure. And what if you do all that and it doesn't work and you haven't developed anything else? That's the kind of life crisis I would do a lot to avoid. It is also where I think the American dream starts to run into trouble. The old American dream of having a house and getting along with the family is fine. The new American dream of being constantly upwardly mobile economically means, I think, that you get a wacky society, the kind we have.

"You can't separate inflation from these things," insists Steve. "Things are so complex now that they all overlap."

91

Steve and Betty sit near one of their few luxuries, a custom, contractor-installed fireplace. Some finishing work remains to be done with the stones, but the cost so far has reached $1,500, and the McColls have decided to hold off on completing the project. Though sparsely furnished, the living room is comfortable; it gathers warmth from the natural wood casements around windows and doors. The McColls could not have afforded the home, even at its exceptionally reasonable $34,000 price, without help from their parents.

The McColls' outlook on the economy is, like most Americans, puzzled, perplexed, and sometimes contradictory. "I have very mixed feelings about government spending," Steve says. "On the one hand, I don't mind the government financing all sorts of social programs. On the other, I do mind the bureaucracy. If we're serious about social programs being run by the government, we should try and streamline them as much as we can.

"In a different way, the same sort of situation exists with the big oil corporations. An awful lot of the huge profits go to top management and beyond. Their control, their monopoly of a number of products, are central to the structure of society that we have."

"The fact is that every industry goes back to fuel," agrees Betty. "As the fuel goes up, everything else goes up. I'm really troubled, not so much by their control of oil, but by the fact that oil companies are the holders of coal fields and uranium mines and have invested in nuclear energy. They're moving into high technology solar energy, which I'm sure means the sun is going to cost a hell of a lot by the time it becomes feasible. It bothers me that this economy has become so monolithic on a corporate level that a small enterprise has a difficult time making its way."

"On the national level," says Steve, "the good times are over, barring some kind of incredible breakthrough in technology that nobody seems to see happening. I remember how it was when we were living in Pittsburgh in the 1970s and the trucking industry shut down at the same time the oil wasn't coming to the gas stations. When you suddenly start to feel you can't heat your home, that you can't move from one place to another, and that the trucks aren't bringing in supplies like food, then you start feeling that things could get very bad and you've got two ways to go. Either you become a very tight community—suddenly all these beautiful human resources inside the soul rise up, and there is brotherhood and sisterhood and everybody runs out into the street and shares their bread—or you have the nightmare scenario—the internal explosion where the population boils over. Myself, I get frightened of human behavior if the food stops coming into the cities and people can't move their cars and the toilets don't flush. Then I realize this has to end. Things just can't keep going up and up and up."

THE SUPER SQUEEZE

"The American middle-class dream—a house, a car, and a vacation—is also the German dream. But I think in Germany

today there is probably more security and less financial pressure on people who want to live that dream than in America."—Axel Fahland, thirty-three-year-old civil servant in Bonn, *Washington Post,* August 29, 1979.

As the nation moves into the 1980s, the aspirations of middle Americans and the realities of a long-term stagflation economy are on a collision course. In a survey of 250,000 college freshmen, more than 60 per cent rated "being very well off financially" as a top goal in life. Their attitudes were more materialistic than those of any recent entering college class, according to a 1980 poll by the University of California at Los Angeles and the American Council on Education. Record numbers reported they were seeking business careers, especially women students, among whom interest in the corporate world more than quintupled from 3 to 17 per cent since 1966, the first year of the survey.

But many of these young people face great difficulty in achieving the success that once came almost automatically to those who ran hard after the American dream. Even if the economy had been expanding rapidly, the corporate career paths of the 1980s were bound to have been overcrowded. In 1975, there were 39 million Americans in the prime promotion 25 to 44 age category, notes Jerome M. Rosow, president of Work in America Institute, Inc. By 1990, that figure will have grown to 60.5 million, in Rosow's words, "an extraordinary rise of 55 per cent."

In *Work in America: The Decade Ahead,* edited by Rosow and Clark Kerr, economist Arnold Weber draws a grim picture of fierce struggle. "Competition to move up the organizational ladder will be sharpened further by the secondary effects of the antidiscriminatory laws, which have brought women and minorities into the privileged corners of the occupational structure from which they were excluded in the past." Whereas there already were thirteen competitors for each middle management position in 1975, nineteen persons wanted the same job by the 1980s and nearly a third were women or members of racial minorities, says Weber.

"I don't believe that we should be forced to accept so many minority groups, so many women, so many of anything. They should be the best qualified people for the job. If this is supposed to be because some people were slaves two-hundred years ago, I don't buy that. I haven't seen any slaves in this country. Somebody has got to point one out to me. I know black people who have stocks and bonds, gold and silver, and drive nicer cars than I have, merely because they got out in the marketplace and competed. They worked. Everybody has to start at the bottom."—Indiana blue-color worker, September 1979.

Women and minorities aren't the only ones crowding the employment picture. Inflation prompts retirement-age workers to hang onto their positions, further intensifying the job scramble. Nearly half of those responding to a Louis Harris poll of retirement attitudes in 1979 said they wanted to work beyond the age of sixty-five. "It is impossible to scratch very far beneath the surface these days," Harris reported to the House of Representatives Select Committee on Aging, "without turning up the dominant worry . . . deep concern over the continuing high rate of inflation."

The white-collar ranks—precisely those occupations traditionally chosen by upwardly mobile Americans seeking advancement—have taken the brunt of inflation's pounding, particularly in recent years. Indeed, only workers who belong to strong unions manage to insulate themselves from the effects of price increases. Moreover, the *relative* gap between blue- and white-collar workers has steadily widened. In 1958, the average autoworker made half again as much as the typical bank employee. Today the incomes of both groups have increased, though by no means equally; now autoworkers are twice as well paid as bank clerks and tellers. In the late 1960s, full professors earned what were considered comparatively high salaries. Between 1967 and 1978, their after-tax real incomes dropped by 17.5 per cent. Similarly, attorneys as a group lost nearly 5 per cent in purchasing power, according to a study for the California Assembly. As sociologist Paul Blumberg observed in *The New Republic:*

White-collar employees now have a double reason for unrest. First, they are no longer making the economic gains they were long accustomed to in the postwar era; often, they are actually worse off than they remember being a few years ago. Second, they are losing ground more rapidly than ever to a visible group of blue-collar workers.

Even so, hourly wages paid to U.S. blue-collar workers, for years the highest in the world, had themselves slipped to fifth place by 1979. Japanese manufacturing workers earned an average of $6.70 compared to $5.63 in the United States. And American business executives finished even lower in the global rankings. A top manager in West Germany could expect 30 to 50 per cent more in base salary than an American counterpart, according to Towers, Perrin, Forster, and Crosby, a New York-based management consulting firm. Base pay for four manage-ment jobs—chief executive officer, finance, personnel, and marketing directors—were compared among companies in thirteen countries. In seven of the thirteen nations, at

96

least half the jobs commanded higher salaries than in the United States.

Moreover, because of inflation, pay hikes for even stellar management performers often are more illusory than real. James A. Giardina and Jonathan L. Pollack analyzed the pay raises granted chief executive officers and top financial executives from 1972 to 1978. What originally looked like a pay and benefit hike of 48 per cent, Giardina and Pollack wrote in Arthur Young & Company's *Executive Compensation Letter*, dwindled away to a net decrease of nearly 7 per cent. Their dismal prediction: "Executives will continue to lose ground in terms of real compensation."

The combined effects of inflation and their own sheer numbers mean many of today's strivers will have to settle for smaller gains in real income and jobs with less prestige. Some may react by hustling harder; more are likely to join the white-collar unions predicted to gain widespread acceptance in the 1980s. Others may simply take the attitude that the hard work isn't worth it and silently slough off. None of it was good news in a society already plagued by growing alienation in the workplace. A Boston University survey of middle managers, the "guts" of most big corporations, found:

• Nearly a third (29 per cent) reported their advancement was falling short of expectations.

• Only 33 per cent felt they had significant control over their own destinies.

"It is going to be one of the toughest times in recent years for the majority of candidates for such middle management staff functions as research, purchasing, distribution, public

relations, personnel, engineering, data processing, treasurers, and generalists."—executive search firm president, *Chicago Tribune*, October 14, 1979.

"Organized work has lost its potential for producing a better life and the aspirations of men are allowed to float off to oblivion."—engineer John Hird writing in *Assembly Engineering* magazine.

"Inflation is the most dangerous, difficult thing facing this nation, because it threatens to destroy an American dream— that everybody in this country has a chance for a step up, to improve their lot in life, that tomorrow is going to be better." —U.S. Senator Lloyd Bentsen of Texas in comments to a television interviewer.

The middle American mood could not have been brightened by the growing burden of the nation's "taxflation" system. Consider the effect of a 13 per cent pay hike (far higher than most people got, but about equal to 1979's inflation rate) on a $22,900 wage earner with three dependents. The raise would boost family income to $25,900, but federal income tax would rise too— by nearly $600 more than the year before. And social security taxes would be collected at the $1,404 maximum. Thus, the 13 per cent pay raise would be cut by nearly a third. The family ends by paying one of every four new dollars it earns to the government and simultaneously loses the race with inflation. *U.S. News & World Report* used the example of a married worker with two dependents and a nonworking spouse whose income had matched inflation, starting from a 1974 base of $20,000. By 1979, the mythical family was making $29,380, but after-tax income was actually $417 *lower* in constant dollars. Why? Because

98

family income was now taxed at a higher rate, resulting in a jump of 60 per cent in federal income levies (from $2,510 to $4,030). And Social Security taxes had nearly doubled in the five-year period from $772 to $1,404. Indeed, by 1987, maximum Social Security payments will have climbed to $3,003 annually, a double-barreled hardship for dual paycheck households which must pay them twice.

"People at work are saying now that it doesn't make sense to come in on Saturdays and Sundays, because the government takes so much out of time and a half and doubletime. It makes it seem like you're not getting anywhere."—auto worker, Trenton, New Jersey.

Taxes especially hurt families in which both husbands and wives work. Indeed, the tax structure, in an ironic parallel with the welfare system, may actually foster marital instability. The reason: the "marriage penalty," the extra tax paid by a married couple filing a joint return compared to what they would pay as separate individuals. The penalty grows as the second earner's income approaches that of the first. In a two-income family earning $25,000, for example, the marriage penalty is $10 if one partner earns only 20 per cent of the total; if the partners contribute fifty-fifty to the income, the penalty increases seventy-fold, to $701.

"Working wives are among the most heavily taxed people in America. They can pay more than the big corporations, who pay 46 to 48 per cent. By the time you add up federal and state income tax and Social Security, the working married woman frequently pays 50 per cent."—Barry Steiner, tax expert and author of *Pay Less Tax Legally*, quoted in the *San Francisco Chronicle*, February 17, 1979.

Because of biases in the tax laws toward one-breadwinner families, there has been an increase—no one knows how much—in the incidence of tax divorce, legal disunion for the sole purpose of escaping the "marriage penalty." Other dual-income couples simply live together without bothering with the formalities of wedlock.

"They are, by their own account, a perfectly happy couple. Yet every winter for three years, David and Angela Boyter of Ellicott City, Maryland, flew off to the Caribbean to get a quickie divorce. The Boyters have divorced three times and remarried twice in the last five years just so that when tax filing time came around, they could reap the benefits of bigger standard tax deductions for single persons." —Washington Post, September 12, 1979.

How did our tax laws reach such a wretched state of incongruity? Partly at least, as a result of efforts to make the system fair. Before World War I, taxation largely consisted of direct levies on property by state and local governments and the imposition of revenue-generating tariffs by the national government. Just prior to World War II, in fact, less than four million mostly upper-income Americans paid federal income tax, and then not very much. Movie stars like Charles Chaplin, Claudette Colbert, and Harold Lloyd amassed large fortunes on their lightly taxed earnings.

With the enormous financial needs of World War II, the federal income tax became a mass tax in 1941, and the question became how to distribute the burden equitably over the moderate- to middle-income range, where most revenue could be anticipated. In early America, taxation focused on real property, based upon the assumption that such a method fairly placed the heaviest levies on those who reaped most of society's benefits. Today, however, government has successfully broken the link between those who reap and those who sow. The tax burden has shifted to the widely dispersed, politically unorganized middle class, at the same time more and more benefits go to members of the upper and lower classes, often organized into special interest groups.

"We have seen over the years the extraordinary effects of what happens to tax rates and tax payments as inflation takes hold. What it tends to do is create an excessive amount of revenue for the federal government. Our experience has been that what they have, they will spend, and a little more. Unless and until the federal government pulls in its expenditures, and also curtails the amount of tax revenues it takes in through the 'inflation dividend,' inflation is not going to be brought down to a point where the average American can live with it." — Alan Greenspan, former chairman of the Council of Economic Advisers.

The combination of inflation and progressive taxation permits politicians to spend more money—thus ingratiating themselves with more special interest groups—without appearing to increase taxes. For the average taxpayer, however, the distinction makes little difference. Indeed, the battering of middle-income families from 1974 to 1979 came at a time when taxes supposedly were being cut, individual brackets widened and exemptions increased. The culprit: inflation, generating more than $12 billion in tax revenues in 1979 alone as it drove millions of wage and salary earners up the tax ladder. Indeed, it has been estimated that a single percentage point of inflation is worth an additional $1.5 billion in revenue to the government. If any doubt existed about the importance of

101

taxation to Uncle Sam, it could be dispelled by remembering that between 1914, when federal income tax initially was levied, and 1978, the United States population doubled and the economy grew to eight times its original size. During the same period, however, federal income tax revenues increased an incredible 676 times, from $266 million to $180.1 billion.*

Squeezed to provide the classes above and below with advantages its own members find increasingly difficult to afford, the American middle class has responded in two ways—first, by becoming smaller in size; second, by borrowing more to maintain its status despite declining purchasing power.

As Gerald Cavenaugh wrote in *The Progressive,* the home itself is no longer "a middle-class haven for raising a family but a setting for a lifestyle which precludes the very thought of children. The middle class thus shrinks even while the demand for housing remains strong."

---

* As we have seen, the burden came in the years after 1940 and mostly fell on those with mid-level incomes. For example, after 1979 adjustments, the highest or "marginal" income tax rates for individuals filing joint returns for incomes of $30,000 a year actually rose a percentage point, while the rates for income brackets from $40,000 to $250,000 were reduced or remained the same at every level. Similarly, minimum $350 tax cuts for those earning $40,000-plus wiped out the increase in 1979 Social Security taxes. In fact, it was *only* the middle income worker—earning from $20,000 to $35,000—who experienced any appreciable increase at all as a result of the higher Social Security taxes. Those making $20,000; $25,000; $30,000; and $35,000, suffered respective net income declines of $107; $162; $98; $36; annually. By comparison, those earning $40,000 came out ahead by $42, thanks to a larger tax reduction ($375) and the fact that the Social Security increase reached its maximum at $333 (the difference between a 1978 top of $1,071 and $1,404 in 1979). Disaffection with Social Security taxes took dramatic form on January 1, 1980, when Alaska government employees became the first state workers to withdraw from the Social Security system. Social Security administrators told the *New York Times* that tax-squeezed employees of 16 other states want out of the federal retirement scheme, meaning 100,000 public workers could be bailing out of the program by the mid-1980s.

Nearly one in two first-time home buyers, Cavenaugh reminds us, are childless working couples.

"Inflation is the big reason people don't have as many kids today as they used to. Economically you just can't afford it. We just have one child and we're glad. Some of the younger students I go to school with have a brother and sister in college too. I don't see how their parents do it. I don't see how you could put three kids through school unless their father is a lawyer or a doctor."—Indiana housewife, recently returned to college.

For millions of Americans, the only way to avoid the inflationary noose has been to borrow on future earnings. Economists estimate Americans carry about 600 million credit cards and devote nearly a quarter of their income to pay debts not including home mortgages. Monthly credit card charges tripled during the 1970s, according to the University of Michigan's Institute for Social Research. "The consumer response to persistent inflation seems to be: why not?" observed William Greider in the *Washington Post.* "Why not buy now instead of later—jewelry, cars, houses, boats, credit-card vacations? Tomorrow it will only cost more, much more."

"One morning you're sitting with the checkbook and a pile of bills and you realize that stretching is not going to work, that the bills are far exceeding the income available to pay them. And you take a look at how you got there. Basically, we married young, I entered into a well-paid profession that I progressed through quite nicely and I think we had more money and more available credit than we really were able to handle. The money came in faster than our maturity to use

that money did."—university systems analyst in interview with CBS correspondent Charles Collingwood.

Americans not only borrowed on their Visa and Mastercharge cards to keep pace with the high cost of living, but also took out second and third mortgages on their homes. *Time* called it "invisible money"; *Business Week* said the U.S. had created "a new debt economy, a credit explosion so wild and so eccentric that it dwarfs even the borrowing binge of the early 1970s."

By the eve of the 1980s, installment debt (exclusive of home mortgages) had soared beyond $300 billion and, as inflation deepened, people took longer to pay back their loans. The number of new auto loans of more than thirty-six months quadrupled between 1975 and 1978. Consumer bankruptcies rose and though organizations like Washington, D.C.'s Consumer Help Bankruptcy Clinic sprang up to help, in the end it was probably other consumers who would do most of the paying. The pinch was on and few were flush enough not to murmur at least an occasional "ouch!"

Notebook 7:

DON OSTERMAN

"This year the issue is economics," Don Osterman is saying. "There is a clear emergency at hand; nobody feels like we've got four more years to play around." Don Osterman, forty-four, is a local mayoralty candidate and spokesman for the conservative American Party. By day, Osterman works at a plant that punches out cold metal stamping dyes for automobile tail lights and emission control equipment. He's seen his own pay go up sharply since he started in the business as a teenager in 1940. "On the other hand, everything I've gotten has been to help me keep up with inflation. I really feel like I haven't had a raise in ten years. I'm no different than anyone else. Everybody has money, but nobody has a future, nobody has anything to hang onto.

"I spoke last week to a senior citizen's group on inflation. I'd spoken to the same group in 1976 but this time people who would not even listen to me before came up and shook my hand. They said, 'He told us more than the Republicans and the Democrats did.' Before I was just a renegade outlaw troublemaker who was trying to undermine the two-party system. This time they agreed with me.

"I think more people are aware of these problems and that's why we're getting the new acceptance. For example, I've been telling the people at work that unless the government puts a gold or silver value on the dollar, there's no stopping this. Two or three years ago they couldn't see it; some of them thought I was a total nut. But now that their money doesn't buy anything, they come around and say, 'Do you think the inflation is going to last another year?'

"I think that realization is behind the change in attitudes, particularly in the media. Before, when we ran we practically had to buy space in the paper. We would take in a press release and they might print a paragraph saying June or Don Osterman held coffee at so and so's house and discussed current issues. Now sometimes we get half a page. The TV station has set us up three times for debates; before we were never invited. The League of Women Voters invited us to their debate, the Chamber of Commerce invited me to address their breakfast; I've got numerous other speaking engagements. In the past, none of this happened, we were ignored."

Osterman's American Party, which accounted for about 3 per cent of the vote in his state's 1976 general election, is a midwestern spinoff of the unsuccessful Wallace White House forays. In his living room three years later, Osterman sits on an orange plastic chair in black slacks and a plain white shirt, recalling the Wallace campaign's racist overtones with distaste. He has no interest in the support—tacit or otherwise—of groups like the Ku Klux Klan, Osterman insists. Nonetheless, the American Party is opposed to forced busing and gun control, wants the government to get "entirely out of welfare," and is against any qualifications other than merit in school admissions, hirings, or promotions.

Lately, however, American Party candidates spend most of their time on economic issues, railing against government spending and inflation. "I think people are shopping for a new party or a new philosophy of government," Osterman says. "The old philosophy has been spend, spend, spend. People now realize, maybe too late, that they've spent too much. The two other candidates just agree with themselves. They're for getting more aid for the city from Washington."

"I say the whole country, everybody in it, is on welfare. They complain about welfare but the only way they can regain control is to cut all federal strings to the police, to the libraries, to the schools. It isn't going to be an easy job and it isn't going to be done overnight, but somebody has got to start the pendulum swinging in the opposite direction."

One of Osterman's favorite themes is that today's dollar is only substitute money. To qualify as "real" money, Osterman tells his audiences, a currency must possess four qualities: (1) intrinsic value; (2) scarcity; (3) divisibility (i.e., usable in standard denominations); (4) durability, (i.e., be able to survive natural calamities such as fire and flood). Old-fashioned monetary homilies, Osterman has found, are becoming part of new-fashioned politics.

Much of what is wrong with America, believes Osterman, can better be understood in terms of history. "We have made the same fatal mistakes that Rome and Greece and Germany and France and England and Bolivia and a number of countries have made. No country has ever successfully survived paper money inflation for more than eighteen years—Germany went exactly fifteen years, 1904 to 1923, and collapsed—and the U.S. is fifteen years into its cycle. What makes us think we're so smart that we'll escape it?"

Osterman holds up a silver coin. "This is a half mark, dated 1904. It bought two eggs. By 1910, one mark could buy only one egg. On Sept. 23, 1923, one egg cost three trillion, 200 billion marks. Postage stamps were overcancelled with values changing so fast that German authorities rubber-stamped them. The cost to mail a letter went from 100,000 marks to 250,000, to five million, then to two trillion marks—just to mail a letter.

"What happened? There was a period, a short period, of turmoil. In the struggle for power a guy by the name of Adolf Hitler had the right people at the right time.

"Okay, you say, but that's Germany, this is America." Osterman holds up another coin. "This is an everyday common issue silver dollar, not a collector's item. It's worth $14 now.* Today we have the Eisenhower dollar—it's not a silver dollar, but a cheap, clad dollar."

"If somebody put me in the White House and said, 'Don Osterman, save us!' I would immediately take the gold we still have and begin minting coins and distribute those coins. I'd close Fort Knox down; the gold belongs in the pockets of the people. That's the only way to stop inflation.

"I am going to tell you what I think is going to happen, God help me, I hope I am wrong. Our money will collapse. It will be worthless. All commerce will stop. There will be no way for my boss to give me something in exchange for my labor. There will be no way for the farmer to exchange the things he has in any quantity. We'll go to a barter system and I doubt very seriously our government will survive as a free government.

* October 1979.

108

"There may also be a period of total anarchy, where people say, 'hey, I think so-and-so has food in their basement, they've got gold in their attic, let's go get them, those people kept it for themselves.' There may be a lot of dead people in this country.

"My neighbors are good neighbors and they wouldn't take anything from me and I wouldn't take anything from them. But one reason we've got a police department is to protect us from the lawless element every society has. The only thing that stands between them and me is the police department. But as part of inflation, the policing powers of government break down. Policemen will say, 'I'm not going to go out and risk my life for no pay; I've got to be home protecting my own property.' If the police no longer function, either because there is no money or because they desert the ship, you go back to the jungle, you go back to anarchy. It has never happened here and we have a hard time believing it will. But it has happened in other places and we are naive to think we are immune."

THE HEAD TRIP

The Middle Class is a class embarrassed about itself, never quite in possession of its pride. It runs from those behind—the failures, the nobodys, the ones who get pushed around and have to swallow it. And it strives after those ahead—where people feel full and self-confident. Middle is a tender and trembling place, full of hope and hurt.—John Curtis Raines in *Illusions of Success.*

Today much of that hope and hurt is entwined, deeply entwined, with the destructive psychology of inflation. Inflation feeds discontent by breaking down the connection between honest endeavor and just reward. ". . . Inflation imposes a kind of lottery on everyone," wrote Robert Fuller of The Worldwatch Institute, "redistributing rewards and penalties rather arbitrarily, and often inequitably. The redistribution may reward shrewd speculation, but it does not necessarily reward hard work or honor reasonable and justified expectations."

It would be difficult to overemphasize the importance of this point. America is, after all, the original incentive economy, the land of the free and the home of the ambitious. The potential of upward mobility motivates the American middle class. As Raines observed, "middle becomes valuable, a significant place to be, only as it promises something ever above itself, or at least appears

110

to itself to do so." Increasingly, though, members of the middle class don't do much moving up; they just run harder.

The old middle-class idea of getting ahead meant participating in real growth, personally and collectively. The eventual goal was usually self-employment, becoming one's own boss and moving up into the next class, if not in one generation then the next. A carpenter's son might one day have his own building trades company and the carpenter's grandson a college education. Inflation has helped change that. For a long time now getting ahead in America hasn't really meant getting ahead at all. It has only meant getting more.

Their pockets bulging with inflated dollars, the American middle class played the crucial role of consumer in a massively expanding postwar economy. By 1970, only 14 per cent of all U.S. families lacked an electric coffee pot, according to *The American People*, E. J. Kahn's review of the 1970 census. Forty-seven million electric hair dryers were sold during the affluent 1960s; three times as many families had air conditioners in 1970 as had them ten years before, and the number of radios per household jumped by 60 per cent. During the same period, Americans paid $180 billion for new and used cars, drove them 312 billion miles and spent $8.5 billion fixing them up.

Americans *consumed*. But were they affluent? Were they adding to their store of real wealth? Were they moving up?

"I think the American people are spoiled. They've maybe got a boat and a camper out in their driveway, but it doesn't mean anything. It's not paid for. The trouble is they want more than they know what to do with."—Midwest farmer's wife, 1979.

111

Rising prices changed the way we judged our own worth, constantly upping the ante of respectability. Survival of one's middle class standing increasingly depended upon one's ability to possess and display things, things of recognizable value, things which others wanted or needed. That meant more demand, and more demand meant more inflation. Labels grew in importance. Consumption became informed, a skill in itself: which toaster was the best, which car had the least defects, which stereo the lowest distortion? A national consumers magazine specialized in supplying the answers. What were these if not signs of uncertainty, wind signals that no one knew any longer what quality or respectability meant? What counted was acquisition of visible proof of one's place in society. Parking a $10,000 Volvo in the driveway gave a greater sense of belonging, of well-being, than putting $10,000 in the bank. Security existed in consumption.

It was not just that inflation hammered down resistance to higher prices, leading to the "buy now" psychology. Inflation did that, but it also robbed our lives of quality. Just as a debased currency cheapens the labor of working men and women, it also cheapens the real worth of things they buy. Most of us are appalled at the shoddy quality of merchandise today. Sewn-together buttonholes, crooked stitching, and enough excess thread to form a fringe are common characteristics of even the most expensive men's shirts. Parts that rattle, malfunction and fail are standard equipment on even a new automobile. Why is it that the latest appliance always seems more poorly crafted than the old one—and proves the point by going on the blink almost immediately? In many cases, the answer can be traced to inflation, and the fact that materials are often the easiest place for manufacturers to cut costs.

As the 1980s began, we stood on the threshold of the

end of things as they used to be. Americans were beginning to perceive that the new inflation was like nothing else before. For the first time and all at once it seemed, the land of plenty didn't have enough of anything, not enough resources and raw materials, not enough "affordable" housing, not enough good jobs for its college graduates. The economy whose backbone was an acquisitive middle class had slammed into a stone wall of limits.

"Prices are a pretty basic kind of information in any society. We all have a feeling that we know somehow what things are worth. Lose that anchor and you feel you've been cut adrift."—Author Martin Mayer, commenting on Public Broadcast System inflation special, May 3, 1979.

They had grown up, taken on responsibility, done what they're supposed to do. And suddenly, it's not okay. They can't figure out why. They say, 'Where the hell is that promise? You promised me, if I was good.' Well, it's not true."—Sociologist Lillian Breslow Rubin, discussing blue collar layoff victims, *San Francisco Chronicle*, April 1, 1977.

Inflation plays games with our minds. It makes victims of us and it makes fools of us. During the early and middle stages of inflation, workers seem to be pulling within reach of their material goals. Then, in a cruel joke, those dreams are snatched from reach. A $3,500 Chevrolet becomes a $5,500 Chevrolet becomes a $7,500 Chevrolet. "Just when I'm finally making enough to get a slice of the pie," complains one worker, "the pie has gotten too expensive."

Can it be surprising when pollster Daniel Yankelovich warns that among one of every four workers, "the American dream threatens to unravel and become a mockery

. . ."? In the 1960s, three-fifths of all employed Americans believed that "hard work always pays off," Yankelovich reports; at the beginning of the 1980s only 43 per cent hold the same belief.

Such attitudes may well underlie the alarming decline in U.S. productivity. "Particularly younger, middle management people are no longer motivated to work as hard and as effectively as in the past," Yankelovich told the National Conference on Human Resource Systems in 1978. "An overwhelming 84 per cent of *all* Americans feel a certain social resentment: a belief that those who work hard and live by the rules end up with the short end of the stick."

"In the summer we probably work something like fifteen or sixteen men at the moving business. This summer more than any other, I was hearing them complain about how their money just doesn't go anywhere. They got their raise but the raise isn't enough. They worked a lot of overtime too. It used to be you never heard any complaints. The whole thing is, it's getting hard to get by."—small businessman in Indiana, September, 1979.

Inflation left workers at all levels with the conviction that high wages, health, insurance, profit sharing, and other benefits were more than job inducements—they were necessary to survive. Their demands soon became tightly woven into the economic fabric. "The new generation of workers and their children were conditioned by a boom economy," the Work In America Institute's Rosow told *U.S. News & World Report*. "They have perceived these advantages as normal. Now these expectations have become entitlements." Workers in all categories are showing "a tendency to hold back, to bargain harder, to demand and expect more without necessarily giving anything more in return," reports Yankelovich. Even in the severe 1973–75 recession (the sharpest downturn since the Depression), a constantly rising standard of living was viewed as a right by more than half the workers he polled.

Now, in its later stages, inflation is threatening many of those entitlements, most important among them the retirement provisions for millions of Americans. "The importance of money essentially flows from its being a link between the present and the future," John Maynard Keynes once said. After our working lives, most of us count on drawing a fixed income based on earnings during our productive years. Inflation overturns those expectations, dumping them out like a burglar scattering the contents of a jewelry box.

"Inflation at 10 per cent, if you are on a fixed income, halves that income in seven years. That occurs within your expected life. An inflation rate of 7 halves it in ten years, slightly more tolerable, but still it leaves you unable to exist at the end of twenty years."—securities company president in testimony to Congress, May, 1979.

Put another way, if inflation continued at just a 5 per cent rate for the next ten years, every $1,000 of retirement income—in constant 1978 dollars—would be worth only $610 in ten years and $380 in twenty years. One of the major new entitlements of today's workers—vested pensions—will be worth little if inflation persists. At 6 per cent inflation, for example, each $1,000 in benefits vested at age forty will be worth only $230 by the time an employee reaches the age of sixty-five.

Inflation is the street mugger of our "golden years". Ninety-six per cent of private pension plans are not even tied to the Consumer Price Index. Moreover, such coverage as does exist is limited and uncertain. The nation's nongovernmental pension system represents one of the largest accumulations of private capital in history. Yet, by the mid-1970s, only seven million retirees were receiving private pension incomes; their average annual benefits were less than $3,000. Because of loopholes, fine print, and exclusions, most workers never benefit from pension plans. For one thing, the typical worker changes jobs too often to belong to—or be "vested in," to use pension lingo—most retirement schemes. For another, many private plans are "integrated" with Social Security in such a way that, while their corporate providers obtain a tax-preferred status, benefits are mostly reserved for higher paid employees.* The result is depressingly repetitious: millions of Americans who counted on company retirement plans are short-changed when they can least afford it—in their low-income senior years.

Because of escalating prices, only 6 per cent of single male workers in the manufacturing industries could maintain their standard of living after retirement, even with thirty years of work under a single pension plan and Social Security benefits thrown in, according to a Brandeis University study. And incomes which did seem adequate at the time of retirement could decline drastically because of inflation. "In fifteen years at a 5 per cent inflation rate,

---

* Dear Mrs. (name omitted):
Your term of service with (name omitted) has been sufficient for you to qualify for a vested pension. In determining the amount of benefit the one-half of Social Security paid for by the company is deducted from the gross pension benefit because our plan is integrated with the federal retirement plan. In your particular computation the amount of pension benefit based on the formula is $72.72. The one-half of Social Security paid for by the company is $99.45. Therefore, no benefit is payable to you from the company pension plan.—letter reprinted in *Retirement Income,* a 1979 publication of the Pension Rights Center, Washington, D.C.

the real value of an annuity would decrease more than 50 per cent," notes Paul R. Dean of the President's Commission on Pension Policy.

"Inflation is a two-edged sword affecting retirement income," Dean told a 1979 meeting of the Commission in Detroit. "On the one hand the value of pension benefits is severely decreased for a retired person living on a fixed income. On the other hand, inflation diminishes the value of the pension funds that are being accumulated in the public and the private sector to pay for future pension benefits." Price increases for necessities—particularly medical care, disproportionately represented in the budgets of most senior citizens—hurt retirement-age citizens most, agreed a National Retired Teachers Association official. "As harmful as inflation is to the purchasing power of the general public," he concluded, "it is even worse for the elderly . . . the elderly clearly are being forced to spend more to survive."

It was always a dream of mine to sit under a palm tree with a mint julip in my hand and take life easy. All of a sudden though, ends didn't meet.—Florida retiree who was forced to return to work.

About four years ago, about the time I thought I'd be able to quit the part-time work, I had to go to work full-time.—Chicago housewife, in her late fifties, discussing her hopes for retirement.

How does the retirement-inflation picture look before the fact? Take an executive earning $40,000 annually. Assuming income and prices increase at 6 per cent a year and the aftertax return on savings remains a constant 5 per cent, he or she would need to set aside 20 per cent of

117

income to provide fifteen years of supplementary retirement funds equal to $10,000 a year in today's dollars. At age fifty, the $40,000-a-year employee would need to save nearly a third of his or her income to achieve the same goal.

Compare that typical private sector example to someone fortunate enough to retire from a government job. Retired members of the military, for instance, receive pensions after twenty years of service, sometimes as early as age thirty-seven. Their retirement checks are fully protected against inflation and amount to 50 per cent or more of base pay. For that matter, all federal employees retire with benefits pegged to the price index. State and local officials are only a step behind. Indeed, lavish police and firefighter pensions threaten to bankrupt some cities; San Franciscans in 1980 plunked more into their pension fund for veteran cops and fire chasers than they paid the same civil servants in wages.

In fact, California may lead the nation with the rewards it bequeaths retiring public employees. Former Republican gubernatorial candidate Evelle Younger, who campaigned in the 1970s as a fiscal conservative, benefits from these taxpayer-provided pensions: $6,600 a year as an ex-Los Angeles County district attorney; $10,200 a year as a retired Air Force Reserve major general; $19,000 as a former state attorney general; $20,000 annually, which he may begin drawing when he turns sixty-five, for his tenure as a Los Angeles County judge. A recent decision by the state's Supreme Court upheld the right of certain officials to a retirement formula tied not only to cost of living hikes but also to salary increases awarded their incumbent successors. Younger—now a Beverly Hills attorney—

has filed a legal claim that would more than double his attorney general's pension to $43,000 a year.

Contrast Younger's case with that of John B. Daniel, a Teamster truck driver who put in twenty-two-and-a-half hard years on the road before retiring with bad eyesight. Expecting a pension, Daniel instead found himself trapped in a "catch-22" ruling common among private retirement plans. It seems that thirteen years before his retirement, he had been briefly—and involuntarily—laid off; his plan only paid workers employed for twenty "continuous" years. Daniel, who eventually fought an unsuccessful court battle, wound up with nothing.

Such inequities, together with a deteriorating economy, cast a deep uncertainty over our retirement years and, by inference, other payoffs we seek from work. Repeated surveys document the steady decline in our satisfaction with all types of jobs. Could that be because we find it impossible to attain the financial goals our labors were supposed to help us achieve?

"The conflict between our aspirations and the difficulty we have in realizing them has had a major psychological result for us as individuals. The economic aspects of our life have become psychologically most crucial to us: most of us in the middle class are thoroughly ego-involved in our occupational and consumer status. Particularly for the middle class male, the stakes to be won through his striving have become very high. The stakes have become his very self-respect, his right to look at himself, his family, his relatives and his neighbors in the eye, his ability to keep on living with himself with any degree of inner comfort, even the privilege of seeing himself as adequately masculine."—Esther Milner in *The Failure of Success.*

119

For all of us, women as well as men, the worsening economy has bitten deep into the psychic rewards of our toil. "Inflation," wrote Thomas Petzinger, Jr. in the *Wall Street Journal*, has "become not merely an economic and political problem in the U.S. but a mental health problem as well. This malaise is certain to spread if unemployment continues to rise and inflation doesn't abate much." According to Petzinger, psychologists report that the standard-of-living sacrifices caused by inflation and joblessness can "contribute to marital discord, problem drinking, reduced productivity or incentive at work, and aggressive behavior, including child abuse and rape."

As Petzinger notes, the relationship between national economic conditions and mental health has never been examined in detail. But when prices rocket out of control and the system no longer provides enough jobs, society's different classes and interests grind against each other in angry abrasion. The ultimate result can be chaos and bloodshed. As Thomas Brom wrote in an article for the *Pacific News Service*, "an each-against-all philosophy is working its way into the social fabric, separating the strong from the weak. Survival in an inflationary economy now requires assets, financial agility, and nerves of steel. Few can dance so fast, or so well, or so long."

Notebook 8:

ANDREW L. BAVAS

The prominent midwestern banker faced an angry Depression crowd of depositors who wanted their money back. Suddenly one man, a Greek immigrant, shoved his way to the front, clutching a wad of bills. In full view of the throng, he entered the bank and made a deposit. The group quickly calmed down and dispersed.

The banker retold the story for years. He would never forget the customer's simple act of courage that long ago morning. Neither would the customer's son, Andrew L. Bavas.

On November 29, 1978, Andy Bavas took a similarly singular step during a different kind of financial chaos. He became the first federal employee to turn down a pay raise. That is, he became the first federal employee to *attempt* to turn down a pay raise. As Bavas found out, it isn't merely unusual for one of Uncle Sam's minions to want less money in his or her pay envelope, it is also illegal.

A small man with deep brown skin and the short, burly build of a blacksmith, Bavas was a $43,248-a-year official with the Department of Health, Education and Welfare. Based in Chicago, he had been temporarily assigned to Northwestern University's Center for Urban Affairs.* In six years with HEW, Bavas reports, his salary had climbed 80 per cent.

"It was always hard for me to understand why all these automatic increases were taking place," Bavas says, "My cost of living increase came in October and my step increase, the automatic raise you get as a federal civil servant, came in November. So often I was getting, in effect, something like a 15 or 16 per cent a year increase—at a time when inflation was running at a much lower rate."

When word came from his superiors that he was being awarded yet another pay hike, to nearly $45,000 annually, Bavas balked. "It was too much," he says. "The job I was doing wasn't worth it. My raise was just another example of how we have institutionalized inflation by legislation and government programs which automatically increase spending. In general, I had not felt that people working at the upper levels of the federal bureaucracy were earning their salaries."

Inflated government salaries didn't just happen to be on Bavas' mind. At the time, Chicago's city council, the Cook County board of supervisors, and the Illinois state legislature, were all busy trying to vote themselves fat pay boosts. California's successful Proposition 13—aimed at curbing such largesse—was getting national attention. "I

---

* Under a law known as the Intergovernmental Personnel Act of 1970, Bavas was assigned first to the University of Illinois as Acting Dean of the College of Urban Sciences and later moved to Northwestern University as Associate Director for Urban Affairs. IPA was designed to facilitate movement between the federal government and various public agencies, especially state and local governments and universities. It includes a formula whereby the government and the hiring agency share the individual employee's salary.

was keenly aware of what was going on," says Bavas, suddenly hunching down in his comfortable leather chair. "I could not understand how so-called public servants could be trying to give themselves raises when you couldn't pick up a newspaper without seeing increasing evidence of worsening inflation. It wasn't enough to simply sit there and say, 'well, I want mine too.'"

Bavas wrote a letter to HEW's regional director in Chicago, saying he appreciated the recognition of his work, but that he was turning the $1,272 raise down. The government, added Bavas, could keep the money and do with it whatever it liked.

A short time later he received a telephone call from regional headquarters. "When they told me I couldn't turn a raise down," recalls Bavas, "I said that's silly, of course I can. You can't tell me there is no precedent for a federal employee turning down a wage increase."

Bavas was wrong. Federal personnel officials in Chicago and Washington could find no other case of a civil servant seeking to turn down a raise. Morever, in an 1893 ruling, *Miller vs. United States,* the Supreme Court forbade federal employees from rejecting pay increases. Behind the high court's decision was a desire to insulate government workers against pressure from superiors who might otherwise control their salary levels and, presumably, their readiness to report wrongdoing.

In his well-furnished apartment—an eclectic but somehow tasteful blend of such diversities as an oak roll top desk; splashes of jazzy art; and the craning necks of clamp-on drafting lamps—Bavas scoffs at the relevance of the eighty-seven-year-old court opinion. "Aren't my civil rights being contravened too?" he asks. "Don't I have a right as a citizen and a taxpayer to turn down a raise? Clearly circumstances have changed, and civil servants are no longer our most endangered species. There are more regulations and rules protecting federal workers than there are protecting the American Eagle or many other creatures which probably are more valuable in the long run."

Convinced he somehow could still successfully win the point, Bavas pushed for a definitive response to his request, in writing. On February 23, 1979, it came: "The law and its implementing regulations do not permit an employee to waive payment of an increase," wrote Christopher B. Cohen, HEW's regional director in Chicago.

Meanwhile, the unusual situation had surfaced in the press, triggering a rash of anti-government newspaper editorials and angering some of Bavas' bureaucratic colleagues. The same day he wrote seeking final resolution of the raise issue—personnel officials in Washington "cut" an HEW standard Form 50, ordering Bavas demoted in grade and transferred to Philadelphia. On April 30, 1979, the day he was to show up for his new job, Bavas resigned.

"I wanted out," reflects the forty-nine-year-old Bavas. "I'd already agreed to the reduction in grade as part of a reorganization plan I fully supported, but the transfer was clearly an attempt to get at me.* There was no way I would move. What did Polonius say to Laertes about friends? 'Grapple them to ye with hoops.' I never turn my back on

* HEW officials contend Bavas signed an agreement accepting a subsequent demotion and transfer in exchange for an extension of his assignment to Northwestern. Bavas claims he was coerced into signing a document which, in any event, was of doubtful legality. On the second point, a source highly familiar with government personnel rules agrees. "Such a practice would not be standard or even permissible," he says. Requiring employees to waive future employment rights in advance of accepting an Intergovernmental Personnel Act assignment would be "directly contrary to the spirit and intent of the law," which was designed to familiarize outside agencies with how the federal system operates. An HEW spokesman concedes "it may be time for Congress to take another look" at the central issue raised by the Bavas case—the legality of a federal worker turning down a pay hike.

an old sweetheart and I never give up on a friend. The people I know here in Chicago are all I consider to be of real value."

Letters poured in to President Jimmy Carter, to HEW offices in Washington and Chicago, and to Bavas himself. "If there's anything a working taxpayer in Minnesota can do to help you, please feel free to call," offered one man; "We need more Americans like you," wrote a woman from Wyoming; "Andrew Bavas for President," penned a widow from Illinois. "Somebody should pin a medal on Andrew Bavas," editorialized Colorado's *Rocky Mountain News;* the *Atlanta Constitution* called Bavas' forced transfer "a shabby deal."

From the $40,000-plus types at Chicago HEW headquarters, however, Bavas heard not a word. "I did get a telephone call from an HEW secretary—she works for one of the high officials there—and she said, 'Andy, I've been in this place for ten years and I know you're right. They're overpaid!'

A liberal Democrat, Bavas remains convinced many HEW programs are vitally important, especially to the nation's poor and minority citizens. But in too many instances, he argues, goals and performance remain separated by a wide chasm. "Perhaps we have gotten to the point where the primary beneficiaries are not the people at the end of the pipe—the disadvantaged—but a whole range of bureaucracies beginning with the overstaffed Congressional committees which oversee the programs.

"In my own case, when I first joined the Feds, I thought the work would have some value. As it turned out, the work was of no consequence. My guess is that between two-thirds and half of the federal executives at my level could have been done away with. All the things you have heard about people turning out paper that is never looked

125

at are true. We generated a ton of paperwork which was sent to Washington and I know first hand some of the material was shredded and tossed out or simply stuffed on a shelf by other bureaucrats whose job was to receive it. The whole thing is self-perpetuating, it has a life of its own."

Bavas' criticism of the federal bureaucracy cannot be brushed aside lightly. For one thing, his own service was extensive and distinguished. Beginning as a redevelopment specialist in the Chicago mayor's office, he moved up to become director of operations research for Illinois' Department of Mental Health and then on to HEW as an assistant regional director. Moreover, Bavas' formal graduate academic training was in organizational theory—specifically, the study of bureaucracy—giving him a unique intellectual perspective from which to analyze the system and its faults.

"One thing I have found is that I'm not very suited to bureaucratic office, really," Bavas acknowledges with a laugh. "We institutionalize ourselves in many ways," he goes on. "Civil servants have institutionalized their working lives through a system in which Congress passes legislation but then turns implementation over to bureaucrats who write rules and guidelines which perpetuate the bureaucracy. We have institutionalized greed; there is corporate greed, bureaucratic greed, the greed of individual citizens. It all comes down to wanting more, constantly wanting more and being unable to make any kind of sacrifice.

"We've gotten to the point where everybody expects instant gratification. Whether its kids with drugs, or writers looking for quick and easy insights or blue collar workers who want their new boats now, not tomorrow,

126

there is a lack of self-discipline all across American society.

"I have a lot of confidence in the essential intelligence and good will of the American people," says Bavas, tugging at the cuff of his blue chamois shirt. "But somebody has got to lay things out for them, to make them understand that you can't have it all right now and your way. We've got to make some sacrifices because our own long term interest depends upon it. The unions have to understand that, the corporations have to understand that, we as individuals have to understand that.

"I think we're in trouble as a nation and if we don't recognize it, we're foolish. There was no more futile gesture in the history of economics or bureaucracy than my own. It was only symbolic; I knew that going in. But some place along the line, someone has to manifest leadership. Eventually, somebody has to break the chain. Somebody has to say no."

THE BIG BROTHER

. . . *the Ministry of Plenty's forecast had estimated the output of boots for the quarter at a hundred and forty-five million pairs. The actual output was given as sixty-two millions. Winston, however, in rewriting the forecast, marked th figure down to fifty-seven millions, so as to allow for the usual claim that the quota had been overfilled. In any case, sixty-two millions was no nearer the truth than fifty-seven millions, or than a hundred and forty-five millions. Very likely no boots had been produced at all. Likelier still, nobody knew how many had been produced, much less cared. All one knew was that every quarter astronomical numbers of boots were produced on paper, while perhaps half the population of Oceania went barefoot.*—from *1984* by George Orwell.

"Government, after all, is a very simple thing," Warren Gamaliel Harding once observed. Naive even in his own time, that was a statement Harding would find impossible to repeat today, when real-life conditions—as well as the calendar—draw ever closer to Orwell's *1984*. Americans live in the shadow of the biggest spending government on earth. In the half-century that separated Presidents Warren G. Harding and Jimmy Carter, growth in government at all levels outstripped the population gain six to one. Between 1970 and 1980, the federal budget grew by nearly 200 per cent. As the national debt soared to nearly one-half of the nation's Gross National Product, interest alone was costing taxpayers $70,000 a minute. Meanwhile, government jobs were being created at a rate about one-third faster than positions in private industry.

If it seems that much of the inordinate growth in government has occurred recently, it has. Indeed, between 1955 and 1965, federal outlays grew by "only" 30 per cent, from about $70 billion annually to around $100 billion. In the decade after 1965, however, federal spending outraced all control, jumping by 500 per cent. Part of the reason was that as Vietnam wound down and

128

defense spending dropped, social welfare expenditures increased enormously.

The number of Social Security beneficiaries grew by nearly 75 per cent in the years after 1965, and, within a dozen years, their average monthly benefits had spurted from $84 to $260. The welfare rolls tripled, the number of Medicaid recipients increased by more than eight million, and the number of people receiving food stamps quadrupled.

By the close of the 1970s, federal aid to state and local government had reached $80 billion—ten times greater than the level in 1960. Indeed ,the growth in payments by Uncle Sam to the folks back home outran the ability of federal officials to administer it, giving birth to the revenue sharing program. All the while, of course, state and local governments were becoming more dependent upon Washington—federal aid as a per cent of state revenue nearly doubled from 21.9 per cent in 1948 to 38.8 per cent in 1978. During the "key growth" 1965–1975 period, combined state and local expenditures climbed as follows, according to Alfred L. Malabre Jr. in *America's Dilemma: Jobs vs. Prices:*

- Welfare spending up 331 per cent.

- Interest on outstanding debt—up 253 per cent.

- health and hospital spending—up 251 per cent.

Underlying the increase in outlays at all levels has been the official conviction, often unstated but always implied, that government spending is *good*. "Government spending is more stimulative than private spending," Tom Bethell pointed out in an October, 1979, *Harper's* article, because the government spends 100 per cent of its money. "Private citizens, on the other hand, will save part of it. Savings—such is the state of the economic art in Washington—are thought of as money withdrawn from the economy and stuffed in a paper bag underneath the mattress."

Governments at all levels seem only to grow, grow, grow. Through most of the 1970s, California alone was creating some thirteen new agencies a year, ranging from the Beet Leafhopper Control Board to the Office for Citizen Initiative and Voluntary Action. The budgets of such entities rose from $215,617 in 1970 to $88.7 million in 1979—a 412-fold increase, according to a recent study by the California Taxpayer's Association. "Anybody here not on a board?" quipped an association cartoon.

At the federal level, a special reorganization task force in the President's Office of Management and Budget in 1977 launched a study of how many programs, agencies and departments overlapped, duplicated or contradicted one another. For starters, the task force found that five separate agencies administer seven student loan programs and six different agencies oversee various federal welfare programs. But that was merely the beginning.

Separate sewer construction projects, representing billions of dollars in contracts, were being funded by the Environmental Protection Agency, the Economic Development Administration, and the departments of Housing and Urban Development, Commerce and Agriculture, according to a Sept. 16, 1979, article in the *New York Times Magazine*. Separate meteorological forecasting activities, employing 20,000 persons at a cost of $625 million, are maintained by the National Weather Service, Army, Navy, Air Force, Bureau of Reclamation, and the U.S. Forest Service.

More embarrassing was the existence of two agencies—

130

the Immigration and Naturalization Service and the Customs Service—within the same Justice Department patrolling identical sections of the Mexican border. Although responsible for the same turf, the respective services use different radio frequencies and are unable to talk to one another. "One agency sets out electronic sensors to monitor the open spaces," recounted *Times* reporter Seth King, "then the other comes along and puts out a second set of sensors, sometimes neutralizing the first set. And, on one murky day back in 1968, the OMB insists, a patrol from the Immigration Service and another from the U.S. Customs Service became totally confused and began shooting at each other."

In a General Accounting Office investigation, eight health clinics—all receiving federal funds—were operating in a single city neighborhood under different programs; none of them had any knowledge of what the others were doing. A survey by the conservative Heritage Foundation turned up 228 health programs, 156 income security and social service programs, and eighty-three housing programs scattered among separate departments in the federal government's executive branch.

It would be one thing if government merely overlapped. The trouble is, especially since the 1970s, that it also had begun to over-regulate, and in areas which until then had been of little concern. The "old-style" regulatory focus had been directed at Wall Street monopolists and price fixers and shippers who tried to short weight wheat. Today, however, the spotlight is on regulation designed to achieve social objectives, objectives such as clean air, civil rights and safe working conditions. Often that means protecting consumers against hazards which—in the past—they were expected to protect themselves.

131

'But I don't want comfort. I want God, I want poetry, I want real danger, I want freedom, I want goodness. I want sin.'

'In fact,' said Mustapha Mond, 'you're claiming the right to be unhappy.'

'All right then,' said the Savage defiantly, 'I'm claiming the right to be unhappy.'

'Not to mention the right to grow old and ugly and impotent; the right to have syphilis and cancer; the right to have too little to eat; the right to be lousy; the right to live in constant apprehension of what may happen tomorrow; the right to catch typhoid; the right to be tortured by unspeakable pains of every kind.'

There was a long silence.

'I claim them all,' said the Savage at last.

Are we moving toward Aldous Huxley's *Brave New World* in asking that government solve all our problems? Clearly, the possibility cannot be discounted. Between 1970 and 1975, as measured in "man-years" by the Congressional Budget Office, the regulatory activity of socially-oriented federal agencies grew from practically zero to well over three times that devoted to traditional areas like transportation, agriculture and broadcasting.

The new bureaucracy included 80,000 workers employed by regulatory bodies such as: the Environmental Protection Agency (created in 1970); the National Highway Traffic Safety Administration (1970); the Occupational Safety and Health Administration (1970); the Consumer Product Safety Commission (1972). Besides the "new regulators," as many as sixteen other offices and agencies have been created since 1970, and the powers of others, notably the Food and Drug Administration (saccharin and other "scares"), and the Federal Trade Com-

132

mission (which recently asked that used car dealers be forced to inspect every auto they sell) greatly expanded.

In a series of 1978 articles, Norman Macrae, deputy editor of *The Economist,* argued that government agencies and the problems they are intended to solve have become locked in an inflation of their own: the more we spend, the worse whatever it is gets. "During the peak period of expansion of HEW," Macrae notes, "health costs rocketed, educational test scores dived, and the welfare system crippled instead of aided its clients. During the peak period of HUD, the centers of cities collapsed."

Macrae used the term "public-sector imperialism" to describe a reform-resistant, free-spending government that reaches deeply into the private lives of its citizens. Watch "public-sector imperialism" at work. On February 12, 1980, the President signs into law a bill called the Dispute Resolution Act. Despite mounting pressure to curb government spending, the measure, whose purpose is to help citizens settle neighborhood beefs, will cost taxpayers over $90 million through 1985. The act creates community Dispute Resolution Centers and Dispute Resolution Advisory Boards, and mandates development of "simple" mechanisms to resolve minor civil and criminal disputes. It is praised by proponents as a way of easing the burden of overcrowded courts; Rep. Henry J. Hyde, R-Ill., feels otherwise. "Backfence fights are a local problem," he insists, "the federal government has no business sticking its nose into such affairs. I don't know what it takes for the message to sink in that we've got to be cutting back instead of adding on."

Government growth can be measured in printed words, if anybody has the time. In California, for instance, changes and additions to state regulations occur at the rate of forty-five pages every working day. The *Federal Register* grew from 9,500 pages in 1950 to more than 61,000 pages in 1978. The complicated language and clauses of many rules only add to the confusion. For example, a recent EPA regulation covering notification requirements for manufacturing new chemicals contained 6,000 distinct provisions, 60 per cent of which were exceptions to other provisions, according to a report by the Office of Management and Budget. Fifty- to hundred-word sentences and multi-syllable words insured that few members of the public could ever understand the rule, OMB said.

The more complex government is, the more expensive it gets. The copper industry will pay $3.5 billion to comply with government regulations between now and 1987, according to the Commerce Department, raising copper prices 43 per cent. As they increase in specificity and number, regulations increasingly require lawyers, economists, and social scientists for their creation, evaluation and enforcement; the sheer number of rules cause different governmental departments to crowd ever more closely upon one another.

Senator Gary Hart of Colorado uses the example of a firm wishing to locate a plant in his state for the purpose of converting oil shale into synthetic fuel—supposedly a high national priority. According to Senator Hart, the company must first obtain eighteen permits from the federal government and twenty from state and local agencies. An additional twenty-seven permits will be required for an employee housing project adjacent to the mining operation. "Surely," Hart says, "the public could be served just as well, if not better, if some of these sixty-five requirements were combined."

Critics called it "the cracked toilet seat syndrome," the tendency for federal regulations to delve into ever more finite rulemaking minutae. By whatever description, compliance costs are generally twenty times greater than the government's regulatory budget, according to Murray L. Weidenbaum, a former Treasury undersecretary. "Every time that the Occupational Safety and Health Administration imposes a more costly, albeit safer, method of production," Weidenbaum writes in *Government Mandated Price Increases, a Neglected Aspect of Inflation,* "the cost of the resultant product will necessarily tend to rise. Every time that the Consumer Product Safety Commission imposes a standard which is more costly to attain, some product costs will tend to rise. The same holds true for the activities of the Environmental Protection Agency, the Food and Drug Administration, and so forth."

Not all regulations are bad, it should be emphasized, and some clearly *have* helped consumers save money.* All too often, however, the growth in social regulation has come at the expense of productivity and weakened the nation's economic strength. Ironically, this often makes more difficult the solution of many social problems closely linked to the economy—persistent unemployment among inner city minorities, for example. Our well-intentioned minimum wage law was meant to protect unskilled workers from exploitation. Instead, the rules make it uneconomical to hire the untrained.

We have grown accustomed to the notion that government laws and lawyers, government regulations and regulators, can and should correct the entire universe of human unfairness, from unsafe factories to psychological damage caused by race and sex discrimination. Life is unfair, John Kennedy said, but that bittersweet wisdom

* Despite automakers' insistence that government fuel economy standards would add as much as $600 to the cost of a typical car by 1985, consumers will be the clear winners in any effort to stretch their gasoline dollars.

died with him. In the 1970s, we became obsessed with the idea of fairness. It wasn't enough that everybody knew you had to add water to your 1936 Ford, or "she'll overheat in the desert." Now millions expected Uncle Sam to do their tire-kicking for them; their columns of recalled autos stretched across the country like abandoned Conestoga wagons.

Justice Louis Brandeis warned us "to be most on guard when the government's purposes are 'beneficient.' The most serious threats to our liberty as citizens, consumers and businessmen, "he said," lurk in insidious encroachment by men of zeal, well-meaning but without understanding." Instead, we accept—and demand—guaranteed protection against everything, from unexpected pregnancy to faulty turn indicators. Sometimes we term it consumerism, sometimes environmentalism, sometimes worker protection. By whatever name, such activities have one thing in common: a high price tag.

Government seems to regulate everything but its own spending. Everyone is familiar with billion-dollar cost overruns in the defense industry, but what about the countless, small-scale examples of lax controls over expenditures and of downright waste?

- After a year of stonewalling, the Department of Health, Education and Welfare finally admits it spent $108,678 to celebrate its own twenty-fifth birthday party—six times more than the $15,000 it originally reported.

- The government initially estimates an expenditure of $65,000 in contacting for ceiling repair at the National War College. When completed, the job costs $1.9 million.

- A newspaper investigation reveals 3,000 free facelifts, breast firmings, thigh tucks and other non-therapeutic cosmetic operations being performed at taxpayer expense each year in U.S. Public Health Service hospitals.

• The government ships free birth control pills to Mexico, according to *San Francisco Chronicle* columnist Herb Caen. But huge numbers of the pills remain backlogged at the Mexico City airport, where they have become a favorite food for gnawing—and, presumably, underpopulated—rats. Taxpayer cost: $167,000 annually.

Senator William Proxmire has made a national sport out of spotlighting questionable government spending—such as an $84,000 National Science Foundation study on why people fall in love and a $27,000 investigation by the Law Enforcement Assistance Administration to determine why inmates want to escape from prison.

Considering the convoluted state of their own police force, however, members of Congress had a hard time seeming believable when they levied criticism at others. Four different patrol services roam the same four-block area of Capitol Hill, according to one GAO study. The U.S. Capitol Police per se—assigned to patrol the actual capitol grounds—was beefed up drastically after the bombing of a capitol restroom in 1971. USCP now fields an officer for every eighteen Capitol Hill residents, giving it one of the highest cops-to-citizen ratios in the world. "That one bombed urinal really cost us a lot of money," one ex-lawmaker sighed to the *Los Angeles Times.*

Efforts to curb government spending and growth, as successive Presidents who have tried to reform welfare can testify, mostly have ended in failure. For one thing, once a government program is underway the spending it generates lingers on, and on. The government's compensation program for coal miners suffering from black lung disease, for example, was launched in 1970 at a predicted cost of $90 million annually. Clearly a worthwhile, well-meaning effort, black lung spending nonetheless has vastly exceeded those early estimates. Benefits already total nearly $10 billion and are expected to grow rapidly, especially since the number of coal miners is projected to double over the next twenty years. Meanwhile, lump sum payments and $508 maximum monthly benefits (raised automatically with the pay of federal civil service workers) have been received by more than 480,000 miners or their survivors, the equivalent of the entire coal mining population in 1950.

Another difficulty in trimming down government is coping with the amazing durability of government agencies and personnel themselves. Bureaucrats are like devil grass; they just keep popping up. There were 236 new agencies created in the post-1960, high government growth era, according to the *Christian Science Monitor*. Less than two dozen went out of business. Or did they? Consider the intriguing case of the Federal Fire Council.

An obscure body, the council operated on a $70,000 a-year budget with the ostensible mission of reducing fires in federal buildings. Then an inquiring senator learned the council held no meetings during a six-year period—a time when the number of federal fires fell by 50 per cent. Disbanded in embarrassment, the council was officially rendered inactive. Or so it seemed until *Monitor* reporter Lucia Mouat dialed the old council number. After a series of transfers, she wound up talking to something called the National Fire Prevention and Control Administration, a newly formed body whose operating budget topped $7 million and whose interagency coordinator just happened to be the former head of the old, smoked-out fire council.

It may be difficult to root out bureaucrats, but it's harder still to root out bureaucratic waste. Mismanagement was so prevalent in the government's $755 million summer youth employment program—already more than twice its 1975 size—that a 1979 GAO report found three of four youngsters, supposedly learning about the nitty-gritty world of real work, either goofing off or not even present when they visited sample urban* worksites. "The program as presently operated is generally not giving many youths the type of work experience they need to increase their future employability" (the sole purpose of the program), the GAO reported.

On the other hand, maybe the kids were just learning early what government is really like. Sloppy clerical work alone costs the nation's domestic assistance programs $1 billion a year, according to the White House; overpayments may have robbed the Aid to Families with Dependent Children program of another $1 billion. The Accounting and Auditing Act—which requires every executive agency to develop approved accounting systems capable of generating understandable and reliable financial information for government officials and Congress—became law in 1952. More than a quarter century later, however, 40 per cent of all federal agencies had failed to comply.

Fiscal irresponsibility starts on the floor of Congress. A June 1980 payroll report showed more than 161 Senate aides—from chief administrators to press secretaries and stenographers—drawing yearly salaries above $50,000. The paychecks of several hundred more topped $40,000.

Nothing, however, could equal the record set by the Senate's very own Finance Committee during the last

* The results were better at rural worksites, where investigators found most youngsters performing useful work in small town hospitals, libraries, parks and schools.

days of September 1979. Long known as an easy touch for well-heeled interests seeking special favors, the committee actually managed, during debate on the White House's windfall profits tax, to give away more money in tax breaks than the levy would raise. The difference came to a whopping $20.5 billion and marked, in the memory of *Washington Post* correspondent Art Pine, the first time a Congressional committee had run up its own deficit.

"What dismayed some observers here was not so much the predicament," Pine reported, "which may be funny, up to a point, but how blithely the panel members put themselves into it without any real thought of what it meant in terms of fiscal discipline. Everyone's pet project was voted in, no matter what the cost." With little debate, the committee took only four days to approve a $75 billion package of energy tax credits, okayed costly energy write-offs for homeowners despite clear evidence they were ill-advised, and extended the ever-lengthening list of categories of oil not covered by the windfall tax. 'It was,' Pine quoted one unamused source, 'like a bunch of college kids drinking beer. It didn't matter how much they'd drunk before. They just chug-a-lugged it all.'"

Even to the casual observer, government skullduggery was more often a case of deep pocket than deep throat. Fraud in federal agencies may total $25 billion a year, according to the GAO. Scandal has seemed a stubborn part of life in government programs ranging from military spending to job training, food inspection, and housing projects. Some of the worst recent abuses have occurred in the General Services Administration and the Small Business Administration's minority assistance programs.

The GSA was originally created to save tax dollars by centralizing government purchasing and supply operations. But by 1978, the agency had, in the words of former director Jay Solomon, become a "wounded animal," riddled with fraud, corruption, thievery, mismanagement and "downright abuse of the public trust."

Solomon himself later was pressured to resign, but events soon proved the accuracy of his appraisal. By the beginning of 1980, some forty persons had been indicted by the Justice Department in a multitude of GSA scandals. Some GSA employees, greedy for even more than their "normal" share of illegal kickbacks from contractors, created a company of their own to rake in more government construction work. Contractors told investigators that paying off the agency was the "way of doing business at GSA."

Perhaps most discouraging, subsequent audits showed GSA officials continued to approve millions of dollars in questionable construction costs, even after the revelations of fraud and indictments. "The audits show that GSA regularly has approved claims for construction cost overruns; continued to do business with contractors who had serious problems in the past, and often failed to insist on its rights to inspect contractors' records," reported the *Washington Star.* In one case, the auditors challenged $532,000 of $579,000 in extra costs claimed by architects and engineers for a Social Security Administration building in Baltimore.

In the Small Business Administration, fully 20 per cent of firms receiving special aid for minorities were actually fronts for white contractors, a recent audit revealed. In CETA, the government's sprawling Comprehensive Employment and Training Program, fraud and abuse have "taken money out of the pockets of the unemployed and disadvantged," according to a "white paper" issued by the Labor Department.

141

"I call it CHEETA because the people are being Cheated," says Don Osterman, the Indiana Mayoral candidate. *"They go out and cut weeds for the city. Have you ever seen anybody get a diploma in weed cutting? What kind of a job are you training these people for? You're supposedly training people for the future, but you surely don't need a federal program for weed cutting. Farm boys can cut weeds. My belief is that the federal bureaucracy doesn't really want the minorities to get ahead. This way they can control their lives, they can keep them under their thumbs."*

The Chairman of California's Little Hoover Commission estimates $1 billion of that state's $4.1 billion Medi-Cal program is being devoured by fraud and waste. Mario Obledo, head of the Health and Welfare agency which runs the program, readily concedes the agency is over-populated with underproductive workers, adding that at $54,000 a year, he himself is probably overpaid.

Obledo isn't the only one. From a time when government was regarded as a poor relation on the job market, offering low pay in exchange for security, public sector employment has become lucrative, especially for federal workers. In both white and blue collar categories, federal pay levels exceed private industry averages, even before consideration of such extras as greater job tenure, longer vacations and better retirement plans. As *Business Week* observed in an October 23, 1978, article: "a growing body of evidence suggests that federal employment is one reason government is a major generator of inflation. The evidence indicates that the structure of government salaries is inflated and that the government understates significantly its true labor costs."

From 1955 to 1977, federal civilian salaries increased about 12 per cent a year faster than relative gains made by

142

private sector workers, according to the Advisory Commission on Intergovernmental Relations. *As of March 31, 1979—before another 7 per cent across-the-board increase—some 54,614 federal workers made $40,000 or more annually and of this group the largest single category received yearly paychecks above $47,000.** Add fringe benefits and the advantages of federal employment become even more apparent. Even self-serving government estimates suggesting that federal white collar employees work more hours than their private sector counterparts, show clearly that Uncle Sam's employees enjoy longer vacations, more comprehensive health coverage, and other benefits in excess of those available on the outside. If pensions alone were reduced to levels comparable to private industry, taxpayers would save more than $1.5 billion, according to a Congressional Budget Office report. "Altogether, federal white collar employees currently receive more compensation in the form of fringe benefits than they would under private sector plans," the study said.

Another problem—one that dates to post-World War II days when federal wages were unattractively low—is inflation in pay due to "overgrading." Some 155,000 salaried employees—11.5 percent of the federal white collar workforce—are benefiting from higher pay and job status than their responsibilities justify, according to the Civil Service Commission. Cost to taxpayers of bloated job grades and titles was estimated at $436 million annually. The commission found that up to 28 per cent of Uncle Sam's middle management team was reaping the rewards of overgrading; federal employees were being

---

* Not included in these figures are high-salaried officials among the 650,000 employees of the nation's postal service, nor a breakdown of the nearly 250,000 military officers whose pay exceeds $20,000 annually.

promoted almost one-third faster than those in the private sector.

"The result of the upward movement of people who prove to be in over their heads, coupled with the immense difficulty of firing civil servants, produces a certain amount of deadwood that never shows up in Civil Service Commission statistics," reported *Business Week.* "Managers solve the problem by simple redundancy: push aside the nonproductive worker and hire someone better to do the job. Thus, every agency has its 'turkey farm,' a low-priority division where the castoffs are forgotten, except, of course, on payday."

In 1970, Congress required that federal pay follow a principle of "comparability," in other words, that it approximate compensation in the private sector. But the companies used in the government's comparison survey are mostly large corporations, where salaries are higher and private pension and health plans routine. It excludes state and local government officials whose pay, though rapidly increasing, is by and large lower. In fact, half of all private sector workers have no company pension plans and one-fifth lack employer-provided health insurance, reports the Congressional Budget Office. "The overall effect of including companies that offer no fringe benefits would be a lower level of benefits in the private sector and, correspondingly, a greater comparative advantage for federal employees."

Career government employees, however, can scarcely be blamed for seeking a bigger slice of the salary pie when legislators all around them seem to be busy doing the same thing. U.S. Senators receive $62,500 a year; more than a third are millionaries. Yet, without hearings or a recorded vote, that "august" body repealed a Watergate-era limit on outside earnings in 1979,* in effect granting themselves a little publicized pay raise. On the state and local level, Illinois legislators voted themselves a 40 per cent pay boost—from $20,000 to $28,000—Ohio lawmakers okayed a 28.6 per cent hike and Chicago city council members decided they were worth an additional 60 per cent each year. In New York City, council members refused to join Mayor Edward Koch in rejecting a pay hike and their salaries jumped by nearly 40 per cent, to $35,000 yearly.

Clearly, one could go too far in bullyragging government into accepting all the inflation blame. For one thing, business, as we saw earlier, has often chosen to take the easy course in following wage and price policies it knew to be inflationary. And consumers played a major role in the price escalation by refusing to curtail unnecessary spending and accept the need to conserve basic raw materials, especially fuel.

Even so, polls consistently indicated most Americans blamed "big government" for inflation* and, all things considered, they were probably right.

"Bring democracy and money together and you will have corruption. I knew a Congressman's aide who drew $36,000 a year and only worked three months out of the twelve. He was simultaneously a fulltime law student in Ireland. I don't know

* Senators now are permitted to earn as much as $25,000 a year for speechmaking services and are under no limit on other forms of income except legal fees. The old ethics code requirement placed a flat limit of $8,625 on outside income, and was imposed as a condition for passage of a $12,700 pay raise—an inflation-popping 28.3 per cent—in 1977.
* A December 1979, Gallup Poll found the public convinced that about half (48 cents) of every federal tax dollar is wasted. Significantly, the surveyors found voters unanimous in this view, whether they were Republicans or Democrats, and despite other differences—age, income level and sex, for example.

how he got away with it, but he did."—tavernkeeper in Washington, D.C.

"I feel sorry for the young people. No wonder they hate our goddammed guts, the way the country's run. They look at the unemployment and they say, 'What kind of system have we got?' The culprit is the federal government. They tell us to buy bonds and save. Then they turn around and just throw money away on the goddammdest things you ever saw."—union man in New York City.

"I started one shop, hired sixteen people and sold it. I gave it up because I got tired of OSHA, I got tired of EPA, I got tired of city taxes and reassessments and insurance. They were telling me where I could build, who I could hire, how high to put my smokestack, what kind of gas to use. Everyday there was somebody at the door to look in and see what we were doing. Have you got enough blacks? Have you got enough women? Have you got two restrooms?"—former small businessman in Nashville, Indiana.

Notebook 9:

JOE MALONE

Joe Malone, mayor of Bordentown, New Jersey, says it all started when Bea Bush was about to retire. Bea had been the sole, part-time welfare director in the town of five thousand for nineteen years, working behind a city hall pay window and handling about thirty adult welfare cases a month. When state officials learned the $2,500-a-year post would be vacated, they decided the small-town approach would have to go. Bordentown's welfare program, they insisted, must provide a waiting room and $500 in petty cash, as well as hire both a full-time director and a case worker.

"It was nutty," Joe told the *New York Times*. "We figured that the two salaries would be about $30,000 and to build a room onto our city building would cost about another $30,000. And $500 petty cash? We only keep $15 for the whole city!"

Confronted with the difficulty of replacing Miss Bush and the new and costly demands from Trenton, Malone and his fellow commissioners hit upon a novel idea. "We'd already asked Bea how many people really needed

147

the welfare," Malone recalls, sipping coffee in his dining room nearly a year later. "She thought maybe three of them did."

At Malone's urging, Bordentown's commissioners created a new program, "Workfare," in which welfare recipients would be required to perform community-service jobs. On August 1, 1978, Bordentown officially withdrew from the New Jersey general assistance program for ablebodied adults.* From that time on, the commissioners themselves ruled on welfare applications and awarded the money.

"We didn't beat them with a stick; we didn't put up a sign, 'Welfare Recipients Not Wanted,' " says Malone, a dark-haired, somewhat stocky man of 30. "When a person came in we offered to help them get jobs, or we gave them community work." Anyone who received money, however, was expected to work off their assistance by washing windows, painting, doing carpentry or furniture repair, or supervising playgrounds.

Bordentown's home-grown welfare program seemed to be a clear success. Within a few weeks, assistance roles began to dwindle. During the following four months, the city paid out only $1,000 in welfare payments, compared to $8,700 for the same period a year before. In place of the usual flow of 120 to 150 welfare applicants, there were only twelve; the caseload itself was cut to two. Even so, the state remained adamant: Bordentown must set up the Trenton-approved system. Malone still shakes his head at the memory. "Here was the state insisting we spend $60,000 to run a program that gave out $1,000 in four months."

* Programs involving aid to the disabled and dependent children were not affected.

"The point we were trying to make was, look, we can run our own welfare program down here better than you can. We know our people, we know their problems, and we know their needs. Just get away from us and let us take care of ourselves. The state didn't want to hear that."

"The real battle had nothing to do with rules and regulations." Malone continues. "It had to do with the state being scared to death we'd be able to do it by ourselves. The issue was much bigger than welfare; this was an example of a community fighting the bureaucracy. The state looked at it as if the South was trying to separate from the Union."

Bordentown was an appropriate site for the first skirmish in a welfare revolution. Founded in 1682, the community was the off-and-on residence of Thomas Paine until his death in 1809. A city of tree-lined streets and well-maintained colonial homes, Bordentown fell into British hands on several occasions during the Revolutionary War and counts Benjamin Franklin and Lafayette among its early visitors. After Waterloo, Joseph Bonaparte took refuge in a mansion he built there, living in the city from 1817 to 1839. Bordentown's stable, hard-working black population traces its history to the Civil War, when the town was an important stop on the Underground Railroad.

From its beginnings, the town has been fiercely independent and careful with a buck. The minutes of a 1739 county gathering included this notation: "Also ye said meeting gave Bording's Town people lve to build a pare of stocks provide ye people of Bording's Town build them at their own charge." City tax records reveal the same frugality surviving into the twentieth century. The following tax bill was paid by William McElhoe in 1905:

149

State school tax	$ .16
County tax	1.00
City school tax	.52
City sinking fund and interest	.24
City tax	.28
City lighting	.38
City smallpox expense	.15
	$2.73

Malone himself, a fourth-generation native whose father headed the fire department and whose grandfather was city clerk for a quarter century, has something of a reputation for a take-action approach to government. When a big garbage outfit refused to lower a nearly $100,000 annual fee to handle Bordentown's refuse, Mayor Malone kicked the company out and Bordentown took over its own disposal—saving the city more than $60,000 a year. A railroad hauling toxic chemicals through town on rickety, derailment-prone tracks, was slow in making repairs; Malone told the company to make amends within three days or he would personally bulldoze the tracks. The repairs were made.

In dealing with New Jersey's welfare bureaucracy, however, the former high school teacher had met his match. The state called press conferences to criticize Bordentown and ultimately took the tiny, square-mile city to court. New Jersey welfare director G. Thomas Ritti declared that Malone had violated the law in directing a local takeover of the welfare program: "His actions meant that the Local Assistance Board, which is required by law to run the welfare program in Bordentown, was illegally stripped of its powers. . . . The fact that Bordentown decided not to continue to accept state funds did not exempt it from complying with state statutes."

Meanwhile, letters were pouring in from around the country, most of them supporting Bordentown's side of the struggle. "What everybody seemed to be saying," Malone recalls, "was 'Let's reverse this trend; let's have less government.' We can do it. I think a lot of people felt, hey, here's one town going against the general trend of increased spending. It was like always being a loser and suddenly having a winning team. No matter what politicians say or do, the ordinary people always end up paying more. They see somebody turning the canoe around the other way, and they say, 'Hey, that's all right.'

"I think there is a conservative tide running through this country," he continues. "People are getting tired of other people spending their money. The number of people paying for it all is shrinking. We can't expect the elderly to foot the bill, but their population is growing. The population on welfare is growing. But the population in the middle paying the bills is getting smaller. How long can we go on paying people for not working, for not being self-sufficient?"

"I don't know what kind of taxes you pay," Malone tells a visitor, "but I know every year it's going up. We're charging people more to take care of the welfare group, but what's happening is the people who are marginal between the welfare group and a little above that, those people are slipping back. A lot of them don't want to, but it's gotten to a point where working or not working, they can get the same thing. We've got to reverse that, so the raises people get allow them either to maintain or improve their living standards."

Without strong countermeasures, Malone believes, the nation may soon slip into socialism, with an all-regulating government attempting to satisfy the needs of everyone. "That's the tendency of large government, anyway," he

151

says. "It wants to do more and more for you and allow you to do less and less for yourself. The people themselves don't want that; they want to fight it, but they don't know how—it's a very frustrated feeling."

"I think that's one reason for the response I've gotten," he adds. "I still get letters—I've gotten something like five thousand since we started Workfare—and I can't remember any being negative. People write things like, 'Keep goin''; 'We're behind you'; 'Stick to your guns'; It's about time,' 'Run for president'. It's unbelievable."

The state's lawsuit claimed Bordentown residents were being denied benefits available to other New Jersey citizens. A state judge agreed; he found the Bordentown program in violation of the law, citing provisions which bar elected officials from administering welfare funds. He ordered Malone and the other commissioners to reinstate the old system.

Bordentown complied but at the same time retained its own Workfare program. "No one signed up with the state program," reports Malone. "You can't force people to do what they don't want to do."

Malone claims the Trenton bureaucracy was Workfare's only enemy; welfare recipients themselves welcomed the plan, he says. Signed affidavits tell of former welfare recipients returning to work, finding new jobs, or simply deciding not to accept welfare assistance any longer. One young woman told a national television interviewer how she regained her self-respect by performing work in exchange for assistance.

"In the beginning, the strongest support I got came from the black community," Malone says. "I was on a black radio talk show in Boston and the response was great. Black people don't like the stigma. A lot of people in this country want to believe most people on welfare are black. They aren't; most people on welfare are white. The only people who have criticized this program have been white.

"When people first immigrated here, the whole family worked to get ahead. I don't care if they were Irish or Italian or Polish, they came here and worked. Then we had a depression where no one could find work, so we created jobs through agencies like WPA. That was a good idea, but now we've taken it a step further. Now we pay people who don't even care about working. That's wrong. It's the wrong kind of philosophy for this country.

"If you drove between here and the Trenton station and couldn't find fifty jobs, I'd give you a hundred bucks. They may not be the kind of job somebody wants, but it's work that has to be done. There are a lot of people out working today that aren't doing exactly what they want, but they are providing for themselves and their families. And they're paying taxes to keep these people who say, 'Oh, I don't want to do that; I don't like that job.' I say that's just too goddamned bad."

Joe Malone thinks it is time to stop making excuses for welfare recipients. One of his favorite examples is what he sees as a double standard for welfare vs. working mothers. "Why is a welfare mother any better than the average American housewife?" he asks. At a time when millions of women with children have returned to the work force, "A blanket statement that because she has children a woman can't work is pure, unadulterated nonsense." The present system, Malone argues, directly penalizes women who might prefer to stay home with their children but must hold down an outside job to offset inflation.

The widespread attention focused on Bordentown's welfare rebellion has not gone unnoticed by area politicos.

Indeed, a recently passed law specifically permits other New Jersey communities to set up Workfare programs of their own. And Malone reports a new, if grudging, acceptance when he calls Trenton. "It's interesting that now when I call state offices they tend to listen," he says. The inscription on a neatly chiseled granite tombstone, planted in front of Bordentown's city hall, adds its own testimony to his words: "In memory of New Jersey welfare bureaucracy, 1978."

THE REBELLIOUS MIDDLE

The crowd mills in angry circles, few heeding the chairman's repeated calls for order.

"Gentlemen, please," he cries over the hostile buzzing of many private debates. "We have heard the majority speakers. We must give those who are in favor of the tax a chance to express their views."

*"It is true," a new speaker begins, "this new levy places a tremendous burden on all of us in this region. But, friends, considering the current state of the economy, shouldn't we be proud that the government has called upon us to do more than our share? Shouldn't we—" The voice is drowned out in shouts of protest—*adopted from an account of a Penn-

sylvania public meeting prior to the Whiskey Rebellion of 1794.

Tax resistance has never been either an unemotional or even peaceful undertaking. According to the FBI, three-fourths of all threats and nearly half of all assaults against federal workers are directed at Internal Revenue Service employees. A less violent form of resistance—tax avoidance—is commonplace. The IRS reports Treasury losses of up to $26 billion a year because Americans fail to report all their income. A general Accounting Office study concluded that millions of citizens—many in low-income brackets—skip the filing process entirely.

Why have otherwise law-abiding citizens become uncommonly rebellious about one of life's great certainties—taxes?

"There are very few of us who believe that we are getting our money's worth for the 40 per cent of our income that is being used to support state, local, and federal governments," answered economist Milton Friedman in an address to the Americanism Education League. "If you look carefully at the language that emanates from tax collectors all over the world . . . the underlying theme is that the government is the master, the citizen the slave, his income belongs to the government, and he is allowed to keep some of it by the generosity and majesty of Big Brother."

In fact, the uprising against taxation accounts for only part of a revolt against the nation's present economic system, the remainder being widespread rejection of what has been called the consumption ethic. Simply put, the first tends to be a revolt of the right and middle-right against big government; the second, a revolt of the left and middle-left against big corporations. Whatever the form of their particular discontent, however, all Americans—liberals, conservatives, third-party members, rich and poor—increasingly seem to coalesce around a single issue: economic conditions must be improved.

"Right now we live in really bad times. It's hard to make a living. You're taxed to death. I know a lot of single people who can't buy homes—it's out of sight, it's unreachable."—young woman explaining why she used her tax refund to join a pyramid money scheme (*Oakland Tribune*, April 13, 1980).

It would be a mistake to interpret the public outcry against corruption and wasteful spending—voiced in such measures as California's Proposition 13—as simply the sign of a new wave of conservatism. Seven of eight Americans are more concerned about how their tax dollars are spent than they are about the amount of taxes they must pay, according to the *Washington Post*. "You can see them down on Cricket Street down there," said one man, commenting on a street repair project in his hometown. "They dug it up first; then they replaced it; and then damn if they don't dig it up again because they done it all wrong."

"The current mood supporting massive tax cuts is . . . largely a citizen protest aimed at incompetent, inefficient politicians and a government that is viewed as unresponsive to the needs of ordinary people," summarized Arthur H. Miller in *Economic Outlook USA*, published by the University of Michigan's Survey Research Center.

After a probing look at the sentiment favoring a tax revolt, researchers at Rand Corporation concluded voters were upset about federal salaries and benefits—an *average* of 40 per cent higher than compensation in the private sector—but they were even more dismayed by the direction of local spending. Citizens, said the report, were particularly angered by the steady shift in resources away from direct-service providers—cops, librarians, and firefighters—and toward vaguely defined support personnel and community organizers.

As an example, the Rand team* took a close-up view of recent budgetary trends in Los Angeles. What they found would have troubled even the most apathetic taxpayer. After an increase in city spending $400 million:

Los Angeles now has more support employees than it did in 1973, and they are better paid than the kinds of direct-service providers they supplanted. Los Angeles voters did not possess this sort of detailed information when they cast their ballots for Proposition 13, on June 6, 1978, but they may have had the smoldering conviction that, over time, they were paying more and enjoying it less.

In state after state, that conviction fueled a wildfire rebellion against government spending and taxation. During 1979 alone, reported *The New York Times*, twenty-two states chopped property taxes, eighteen reduced income taxes, fifteen cut sales taxes, eight voted spending limits, and twelve repealed or reduced assorted other taxes. Indeed, half of all states now boast limits of some form on spending. "The movement has struck in urban states (California) and rural (Idaho)," reported the Rand researchers, "in states where the constitution permits voter-initiated amendments (Colorado) and those where it does not (Tennessee), in states with historically low tax levels (Indiana) and traditionally high ones (Alaska)."

Tax cuts, loosely justified on the assumption they will

---

* The $180,000 study project, co-funded by the Ford Foundation, was conducted by an interdisciplinary research group led by economist Anthony H. Pascal and regional planner Mark D. Menchik.

force curtailments in government spending and thereby curb inflation, have become the rallying point for the revolt of the right. The difficulty is that tax reductions, by themselves, can worsen the very illness they seek to cure. "If we cut taxes without cutting government spending," warns author Howard Ruff, "the government will still continue to spend the same amount of money, it will merely be printing press-created money, and the tax revolt, in my opinion, will be highly inflationary." Nonetheless, when most Americans thought about economic reforms, the first thing that came to mind was a healthy slice in their own tax bills.

Consider some of the inflation-fighting economic reforms, frequently suggested in the past, upon which increasing numbers of Americans—labor union representatives, economists, stock market analysts, politicians, and ordinary citizens—agreed:

• TAX REFORM   It seems a fair enough proposition that the tax base should include all sources of income and exclude all expenses incurred in obtaining it. The trouble is that what sounded like an equitable idea hasn't worked out that way. Indeed, anyone who still believes the present system is fair and equal should study the returns of those with incomes above $200,000 who, year after year, pay no taxes at all.

Some have suggested that a flat tax of about 16 per cent replace the present progressive system. Under such a plan, no deductions would exist and income would be taxed at the same rate regardless of the source. The practical chances of enacting a flat rate tax are small. What is imperative, however, is that present income taxes incorporate some form of indexing to better protect middle-income taxpayers against inflation. "Indexing" would tie tax increases to gains in real as opposed to inflationary income, ending the penalty now attached to job advancement as well as the inflation payoff for Uncle Sam.

• WELFARE REFORM   Almost everybody is unhappy with welfare. For most ordinary taxpayers, the issue long since ceased being whether they agreed with the social programs undertaken by their government. In painfully immediate terms, the issue is that they no longer feel able to afford them. When millions of middle-income Americans have curtailed their own plans for children, officially subsidizing continued expansion of the welfare population is difficult to defend. The present welfare system, its destruction of pride and family stability, its fostering of institutional dependency, is a national shame.

That system could be replaced by one which: actively encouraged productive work by its beneficiaries and actively discouraged its own growth. In its simplest form, such a system might consist of a negative income tax, triggered automatically when family income fell below a predetermined level. Recipients could not collect unless they were working, either for private employers or in public service jobs created for the purpose. The negative tax would be added to their paychecks in the same way withholding currently is deducted. Federal payouts for housing, health, food, and almost all other subsidies could be incorporated in negative tax payments.

• DEFENSE SPENDING   Perhaps the most directly inflationary of all government expenditures, military outlays vastly expand the amount of dollars in circulation without producing goods consumers can purchase. Mili-

159

tary waste is legendary* and military spending distorts the geographic distribution of federal funds, redistributing tax money from the upper Midwest and Northeast into the South and Southwest. Indeed, three out of four residents of the nation's 435 congressional districts pay out more for defense in taxes than is ever returned to their areas in the form of government spending, according to one study.

As long-time defense-spending foe Norman Cousins wrote in *Saturday Review* on January 20, 1979:

> The spending of military money has become an end in itself. We have allowed ourselves to believe that having a bigger military budget than the Russians is proof of our national strength and purpose—regardless of the fact that a large portion of our money is being spent on maintaining three separate military establishments with colossal overlapping of authority, functions, and equipment . . .

One defense-spending reform supported by Cousins and just about every other critic is an end to the presence of U.S. ground forces in Europe. The spectacle of struggling American taxpayers being asked to defend the far more prosperous economies of Western Europe should mercifully come to a close.

● FEDERAL DEFICITS A recent Gallup poll showed Americans 6–1 in favor of a constitutional amendment requiring a balanced budget; a majority of the required thirty-four states have approved resolutions calling for a convention to consider such a proposal. Meanwhile, the

---

* At an Army base in Georgia, for example, twenty-three trucks worth $45,000 each were used for target practice. "Although base officials deny it," wrote Jack Anderson in a November 30, 1978 column, "defense records show eighteen of the trucks were in running condition and the other five needed only minor repairs to make them useful as trucks instead of targets."

National Tax Limitation Committee, a group of conservative businessmen and economists, has proposed what may be a more moderate and effective approach. The committee's plan would tie federal spending to the gross national product: Congress could not increase spending by a larger percentage than the most recent increase in GNP. Whenever inflation exceeds 3 per cent, the restrictions would become more severe. The limits would be removed entirely in case of war or similar national crisis.

• GOVERNMENT REGULATION *"Put in an acoustical ceiling to cut down noise;" a federal job-safety agency ordered a Virginia poultry processor. He did.*

"Take out that ceiling—it's a sanitation hazard," said Agriculture Department inspectors. He did.

"No ceiling? Then make your workers wear earmuffs, or you'll be fined," said the job-safety people. He did.
> —*Christian Science Monitor*, May 28, 1976

One solution to overregulation of the present economy might be creation of a new, multi-purpose "Superbureau." Federal agencies, such as the Occupational Safety and Health Administration, could be combined with the Environmental Protection Agency in a more streamlined U.S. Bureau of Regulations. This would be accompanied by laws making it easier to fire and transfer civil-service workers as well as to encourage rotation, especially of white-collar workers, between government and private industry. Businesses could deal with a single federal agency in obtaining permits and approvals. Such an agency would have less motivation to expand constantly into ever more minuscule areas of regulation. It would also reduce overlapping administrative functions, instances of field inspectors from separate agencies tripping over one

161

another at the same worksite, and, hopefully, the issuing of regulations merely to insure an agency's continued existence.

• TAX-BASED INCOMES AND PRICES POLICY "TIPP," as it is called, simply means a tax incentive to keep wages down, by imposing penalties on inflation's two biggest private-sector partners—big business and big labor. TIPP would come into play whenever pay hikes or prices exceeded previously established guidelines. Workers would pay an income surcharge tax on the amount their wages topped the limit; companies would be taxed on excessive price hikes. TIPP proponents argue the policy would have the effect of forcing manufacturers to spend more on research and development to reduce the effect of higher raw-material costs. The policy could be enacted as a standby, "on the shelf" measure, automatically triggered whenever inflation rose above a predetermined level.

"If you don't want much, and don't get much, you can nearly always get whatever you want. . . . We're talking about quality, the kind of quality that money would like to buy. Time to do your work well enough to be proud of it. Few enough things to have fine ones and take good care of them. Time for an occasional original idea and time to follow it. Time for family"—Stewart Brand.

There is another rebellion, quieter but far more profound than the revolt over taxes and government spending. By the millions, Americans are learning to appreciate the simple life. According to a Harris poll:

162

- By 76 to 17 per cent, Americans favor "learning to get our pleasure out of nonmaterial experiences" rather than "satisfying our need for more goods and services."

- By 79 to 17 per cent, Americans favor "teaching people how to live more with basic essentials" rather than "reaching higher standards of living."

- By 66 to 22 per cent, Americans favor "breaking up" excessively large public and private institutions and "getting back to more humanized living" rather than "developing bigger and more efficient ways of doing things."

Were those who responded merely echoing what they thought were "correct" attitudes? To some extent, perhaps. Indeed, some critics suggested the 1978 poll might have turned up the same answers in 1950 as it did nearly thirty years later. Even so, evidence suggests Americans are making a serious effort to alter their lifestyles. Consider the results of a Stanford University survey of nearly one thousand California homeowners, presented at a 1980 meeting of the American Association for the Advancement of Science:

- Forty-one per cent recycled most or all of their newspapers.

- Forty-three per cent changed the oil in their cars themselves.

- Sixty-five per cent had learned self-reliance skills such as carpentry, plumbing, or auto repair.

163

• Forty-four per cent, on at least one occasion, had swapped goods or services instead of paying with money.

• Twenty per cent had a compost pile for use in organic gardening.

Another indication that at least some Americans are becoming concerned with leading simpler, more efficient lives, is the steady decline during the late 1970s in domestic energy consumption. Motorists may balk at driving fifty-five-mph and turning down their thermostats, but they are buying smaller autos and insulating their homes. The results are beginning to emerge and they are impressive. In 1978, America consumed just 5 per cent more energy than it did in 1973; in 1979, the nation's per capita energy usage fell while that of most Western European countries recorded an increase.

Social scientists now report many people who aren't poor are leading lives of "Voluntary Simplicity"—learning to live more simply and frugally, cutting down on consumption, and saving energy. SRI International (formerly Stanford Research Institute) in Menlo Park, California, a business-oriented research group, estimates "VS" has already attracted four to five million full-time adherents and could be embraced by over thirty million Americans by the mid-1980s.

Five principles are identified as central to the "VS" movement:

• Material simplicity—leading a nonconsumerist lifestyle focused upon reducing frills and luxuries in favor of the inner joy of simple living.

164

• Human scale—a preference for human-sized living and working environments.

• Self-determination—raising one's own vegetables, doing one's own home repairs, in general being less dependent.

• Ecological awareness—being knowledgeable of the interconnectedness of people and resources.

• Personal growth—more freely exploring one's own inner potential.

"VS" could create a social order that is "as different from the present as the industrial era was different from the Middle Ages," argue SRI researchers Duane Elgin and Arnold Mitchell. They have alerted business clients that a large future market may exist for goods which emphasize simple quality and durability—wood furniture, well-made tools, self-help medical items, and natural-fiber clothing. SRI's study on Voluntary Simplicity reportedly raised more interest among institute subscriber-clients than any previous report of its kind. Indeed, so intense was the response that senior staffers were dispatched to detail the report for business groups in half a dozen major U.S. cities.

Mitchell and Elgin believe that one of the main forces pushing many Americans toward VS is a reaction against the increasingly complicated nature of our lives. "We have created social bureaucracies (at the federal, state, and local levels) of such extreme levels of scale, complexity, and interdependence," they wrote in *The CoEvolution Quarterly*, "that they now exceed our capacity to comprehend and, therefore, to manage them . . . we are becoming an excessively overregulated society . . ."

Critics argue the Voluntary Simplicity movement isn't voluntary at all, that it has been forced upon its adherents by spiraling inflation. Yet most of those adopting the VS lifestyle did not do so for economic reasons; they are highly educated mainstream men and women who simply tired of the rat-race existence of their former lives. Other prominent supporters have been "turned-off" middle- and upper-class young.

Voluntary Simplicity has attracted at least some supporters in the business community. In the San Francisco Bay Area, a group of alternative businesses have joined forces as the Briarpatch Network. The network offers professional advice in areas such as finance, advertising, insurance, and accounting to its membership, mostly small firms—food and clothing stores, "little" book and magazine publishers, small-scale manufacturers, child-care centers, and the like.

Briarpatch businesses set prices according to their own economic version of the Golden Rule: "The best price is what you would charge your friends." Formal titles such as "president" are generally dispensed with, and profits, if any, are often recycled to help other Briarpatch projects.

"If you reduce the amount of money you feel you have to earn, you'll have a lot more freedom to do the things you love, and more freedom to spend time with the people you love. . . . Money is something society pays people to do what the society—or certain members of the society—want to be done."—Briarpatch founder Michael Phillips in *Medical Self-Care* magazine, Winter 1979–1980.

Whether we agree with the "VS" philosophy or not, there is much to be said for the simple life in terms of easing the burden of high prices. Doing for oneself can take many forms:

• Do-it-yourself doctoring and lawyering kits are helping many Americans save money. Hundreds of books have been published in recent years to help consumers cut their medical bills. Stethoscopes, otoscopes [the instrument doctors use to examine ears], blood-pressure cuffs, and other simple medical tools are being sold for home use, not to mention widely advertised self-administered early pregnancy tests. Low-cost legal kits similarly offer help to individuals who wish to write their wills, dissolve their marriages, adopt children, change names, go bankrupt, or settle an estate. In some cases, the kits are sold by attorneys who step in if people get in over their heads.

• Smart shopping means learning to shop in at least two competing stores, buying when the price is right and then in quantity, and *always* comparing price and size to get the lowest possible cost per unit. Thousands of Americans are clipping coupons and sending in for manufacturers' refunds. Refunders have become something of a cult, their numbers growing in size as prices spiral. Circulation of *Refundle Bundle*, a Yonkers, New York-based newsletter which lists hundreds of refund offers, has grown from thirteen friends of publishers Stephen and Susan Samtur to thirty thousand subscribers nationwide.

The purchase of durable items can mean a big reward for the smart shopper. In general, the three weeks from Christmas to mid-January are the best time to look for clothing, big appliances, and furniture. Auto dealers say the optimum time to buy a car is after New Year's, especially on a day when the weather is bad.

• Taking care of your money may mean forgetting some supposedly inflation-wise advice of the late 1970s. Too many Americans used the "buy now" psychology as an excuse to go too far into debt—not only for homes but for other "big-ticket" items as well. Much of this borrowing was done with the full blessing of "experts" who urged everyone to plunge ahead and pay off their loans later with cheaper dollars. Better advice for the near future might be to remain as liquid as possible, especially if the economy worsens.

One way to protect your financial interest is to shelter as much income as legally possible from the tax collector. Earnings from employee contributions to company pensions, profit sharing, or thrift plans, for example, are tax deferred until withdrawal. Money invested in individual pension plans—Keogh plans for moonlighters and the self-employed, Individual Retirement Accounts for those unable to participate in company retirement programs—is shielded from current taxes. Some annuities may be purchased in single payment outlays of under $2,000 and interest accumulates untaxed.

Most tax shelters—municipal bonds, limited partnerships, and government securities, to name a few—don't make sense for average-bracket wage and salary earners. Still, every little bit helps. For example, someone in the 25 per cent bracket who wants to put away $1,000 a year can save the entire sum in an IRA. In a regular savings account Uncle Sam's slice would be $250, before the investment.

"I remember when the banks closed in 1933. A loaf of bread was just a nickel, but you had a hard time getting the nickel to

get the loaf of bread with. It was actually 1937 or 1938 before things began to level off where you could just go out and get a job. Times were tough. In the early part of the Depression, my dad bought a new car and wrote a check for it. That was our first hint of what the banks were going to do. They didn't want to honor that check, but my dad wouldn't leave until they did. We got out of there when the bank closed at 4:00 P.M. The next morning it was shut down, the doors all blocked off. Dad had taken out all he had, which wasn't much. He always said when he withdrew his money, he broke the bank."—a retired Indiana businessman.

The businessman's father may have enjoyed joking about his role in closing the bank, but as he well knew, forces far outside his control were actually to blame. It is deceivingly easy to overestimate the role of the individual in economic events. And, helpful steps as they individually may be, planting vegetable gardens and learning to tune our cars are reactions rather than answers to inflation. The problems of today's price escalation and unemployment are so complex and the causes and symptoms so interrelated that only concerted effort by our national leaders offers any real hope of providing a longterm solution.

"It's OPEC, it's the farm situation, it's such a combination of complicated things I would never say there's a villain. I'm a little piece of it, you're a little piece of it, government is a piece of it, business is a piece of it. Like Kennedy used to say, 'We all hold office.' "—Esther Peterson, President's advisor for consumer affairs, Carter Administration.

Left unrepaired, a crumbling economy can make losers of everyone. It threatens an angry showdown between

169

those who support themselves with their own labor and those, rich as well as poor, who have grown dependent on their fellow taxpayers for assistance. "The final quarter of the century is going to be a different ball game than the postwar boom," one liberal economist warned the *Wall Street Journal*. "It is the stalemating of the American dream." John Maynard Keynes, the man many regard as the "father" of inflation, put it more simply. Once out of control, he said, the system "engages all the hidden forces of economic law on the side of destruction, and does it in a manner which not one man in a million is able to diagnose."

Epilogue

MUNCIE, INDIANA
"MIDDLETOWN, U.S.A."

The time he covered a speech by Robert Lynd remains a vivid memory for Ed Satterfield, even though it happened more than half a century ago. The year was 1938 and Lynd and his wife Helen were already famous as co-authors of *Middletown* and *Middletown in Transition,* the classic sociological texts which used Muncie, Indiana, to typify the "average" American city. Satterfield had one of his first big assignments as a cub reporter for the *Muncie Star;* Lynd was in town to help dedicate a new housing project.

"He was a white-haired man, very personable," recalls Satterfield, now public information officer at Muncie's Ball State University. "But when Dr. Lynd gave his address, he just sailed over everybody's head. I got back to the office and I didn't know what to make of any of it. I got real scared. My city editor said just do the best you can, probably nobody else knew what he was talking about either. So that's what I did and it came out all right."

Muncie residents frequently have been puzzled by the social scientists who have scrutinized their town since the Lynds first visited in 1924. To its citizens, Muncie simply happens to be the pleasant community in which they live and work and raise their families. But even to a casual outsider, who strolls among Muncie's renovated downtown shops, or leafs through a magazine in the city's colonnaded Carnegie library, or drives past the long stretch of neon-lighted franchise restaurants on McGalliard Road, Muncie exhibits a kind of universal recognizability—it could be Anywhere, U.S.A. Muncie is, as *Time* once said, the town that became famous for being ordinary. It also is the city where, in the fall of 1979, many of the interviews were conducted for this book.

Nineteen miles square, Muncie squats as flat as rolled iron in northeastern Indiana, a 90,000-population city of tree-lined streets; of dark, red-brick houses that somehow remind a visitor of certain neighborhoods in New Jersey; of rich, farmland soil, and of the winding banks of the White River, the main waterway that meanders through the heart of town. Because of its flatness, Muncie could be boring; the sky, always changing, shifting patterns and composition, saves it. Clouds patch over the blue like handfuls of clay, then darken in drenching rain, then fall away to let in the sun.

Muncie is a working town. It is a town of shoved-up sleeves and shirtbacks stained with oil and factory sweat and sturdy leather boots made to stand hours of abuse on the assembly line. The tavern outside the city's biggest private employer, the Chevrolet plant, is called, "Workman's Bar." In the mornings, streets like Jackson and Walnut and Kilgore and Wheeling are jammed with office help and factory hands and college teachers hustling to their jobs.

172

Not only is "Middletown" busy, most of the time it is busy in a wide variety of work. Nearly 170 manufacturing concerns operate in Muncie, making everything from auto transmissions to storage batteries to iron forgings and steel wire. Even so, the biggest single employer is Ball State University, the bustling, working-class campus that carries the name of the town's leading industrial family. And the Muncie area's 200,000 acres of farms are important as well, providing a rich harvest of corn and soybeans and wheat, as well as space to raise hogs and beef.

Muncie means middle. Nearly twice as many households occupy the $18,000 national median income range as any other earning category. Visible disparities in wealth seem soft-edged in Muncie. The area above Ball State, bracketed by Tillotson and Riverside avenues, contains a small cluster of elegant homes, but it is no Bel Air. At lunch in the recently refurbished Roberts Hotel, Edmund F. Ball, former chairman of Ball Corporation, a Fortune 500 company that for most of this century has been the leading economic influence in Muncie, mingles with local shop-keepers and college professors who know him only as "Ed." White folks are still welcome, on warm Indiana summer evenings, to eat a late dinner of spare ribs in Muncie's black community.

None of this is to say that Muncie lacks problems. Blacks who grew up here hold bitter memories of restrictive bank loan policies and other forms of discrimination which survived into the 1960s; their youngsters, like minority youth around the country, find it hard to get jobs. Among whites too, unemployment—reflecting the city's close economic ties to the troubled auto industry—remains stubbornly high. And not a few Ball State professors find Muncie's very middleness a drawback—the town is a cultural and intellectual desert, they complain.

Yet for all that, Muncie remains a kind of national preserve, uniquely un-unique, a place, a whole town, where many of us still see something of ourselves as a community. Even in the nineteenth century, Muncie closely resembled the society described by Tocqueville, a center of an area of almost universal literacy and property ownership, peopled by small farmers. Change came in 1887 when the discovery of natural gas turned Muncie into a manufacturing city; by the time the Lynds arrived, Muncie had moved into a new industrial age.

In one important way, however, life in Muncie differs from the experience of many Americans, or at least those who dwell in urban areas. Its values are still traditional enough, the city itself small enough, so that Muncie retains a sense of humanity and continuity so often missing in larger communities.

Indeed, perhaps the most intriguing finding of *Middletown III*, a major University of Virginia-Brigham Young study in progress, was how *little* life in Muncie had changed between 1924 and the late 1970s. "Viewed externally, the life situation and daily routine of Middletown's young people today are closer to those of their grandparents in the 1920s than were the Lynds' subjects to *their* grandparents in the 1870s," observed the researchers. In replicating most of the questions the Lynds had asked Muncie teen-agers a half-century before, the Virginia–BYU researchers turned up surprising similarities. Fifty per cent agreed that "the Bible is a sufficient guide to all problems of modern life." Three of four of the adolescents—all high school students, some of them grandchildren of the Lynds' subjects—accepted the notion that the United States is "unquestionably the best country in the world"; the same 47 per cent as in 1924 said "it

174

is entirely the fault of a man himself if he does not succeed."

To be sure, change has taken place in Muncie. *Middletown III* researcher Penelope Canan Austin found a burgeoning federal presence "which defies simple explanation" and certainly would have been unknown in the 1920s. They may believe their Bibles, but Middletown teen-agers can exhibit the same foolish smugness of young people anywhere; somehow they find money for big cars and gasoline and, in the evenings, gun their motors and blast their radios as they race on fat tires up Madison Street. Unions have vastly narrowed the differences between workers and what the Lynds called the "business class." There is far greater toleration of racial and ethnic differences today and, finally, women in Muncie play a larger role than they did when Helen Merrell Lynd questioned them nearly seventy-five years ago.

Even with these changes, the scale of the town remains human and intimate. On a bus ride to Ball State University, the veteran driver, a man named Pete, chats amiably with an attractive, white-haired woman passenger about gardening. Suddenly, Pete pulls the bus over to the side, opens the air-locked door, and points to a handsome neighborhood garden. The object of his special adoration, he tells the woman, is a circular plant he identifies as "Chinese cabbage."

The big vehicle remains perched on the shoulder of the road while the driver continues his paean to green thumbery. The passengers sit calmly in their seats, not one raising an angry voice or demanding that the bus move on. There is a long moment when, in all the universe, there is only the sound of the driver's voice, easy, casually friendly, and the interruption, through the open door, of birds chirping in the field, their bright voices floating on the warm, mid-morning September air. The visitor, fresh from New York, Washington, and other important tension centers, stifles his instinctive irritation and relaxes. They may be ordinary, he decides, but the virtues of life in the middle can be real all the same.

SELECTED BIBLIOGRAPHY

BOOKS

Bledstein, Burton J. *The Culture of Professionalism* (New York: W. W. Norton and Company, 1976).

Coles, Robert. *The Middle Americans* (Boston: Little, Brown and Company, 1971).

Fellman, Gordon, and Brandt, Barbara. *The Deceived Majority: Politics and Protest in Middle America* (New Brunswick, N.J.: Transaction Books, 1973).

Fellner, William, ed. *Contemporary Economic Problems, 1979* (Washington, D.C.: American Enterprise Institute, 1979).

Friedrich, Otto. *Before the Deluge* (New York: Harper & Row, Publishers, 1972).

Galbraith, John Kenneth. *The Affluent Society* (Boston: Houghton Mifflin Company, 1958).

Hobbs, Charles D. *The Welfare Industry* (Washington, D.C.: The Heritage Foundation, 1978).

Holcombe, Arthur N. *The Middle Classes in American Politics* (Cambridge, Mass.: Harvard University Press, 1940).

Kahn, E. J., Jr. *The American People* (New York: Weybright and Talley, 1973).

Katona, George, and Strumpel, Burkhard. *A New Economic Era* (New York: Elsevier-North Holland, Inc., 1978).

Kerr, Clark, and Rosow, Jerome M., eds. *Work in America: The Decade Ahead* (New York: Van Nostrand Reinhold Company, 1979).

Levison, Andrew. *The Working-Class Majority* (New York: Coward, McCann and Geoghegan, Inc., 1974).

Lynd, Robert S., and Lynd, Helen Merrell. *Middletown: A Study in Modern American Culture* (New York: Harcourt, Brace and Company, Harvest Books, 1956).

Milner, Esther. *The Failure of Success* (St. Louis: Warren H. Green, Inc., 1968).

Mills, C. Wright. *White Collar* (New York: Oxford University Press, 1951).

Mitchell, J. Paul, et al. *Working in Middletown* (Muncie, Ind.: Indiana Committee for the Humanities, 1976).

Morison, Samuel Eliot. *The Oxford History of the American People* (New York: Oxford University Press, 1965).

Pension Rights Center. *Retirement Income* (Washington, D.C.: Pension Rights Center, 1979).

Raines, John Curtis. *Illusions of Success* (Valley Forge, Pa.: Judson Press, 1975).

Robertson, Ross M. *History of the American Economy* (New York: Harcourt, Brace and Company, 1955).

United States League of Savings Associations. *Homeownership: Affording the Single-Family Home* (Washington, D.C.: United States League of Savings Associations, 1978).

———. *Homeownership: Realizing the American Dream* (Washington, D.C.: United States League of Savings Associations, 1978).

Warren, Donald I. *The Radical Center* (Notre Dame, Ind.: University of Notre Dame Press, 1976).

Weidenbaum, Murray L. *Government Mandated Price Increases* (Washington, D.C.: American Enterprise Institute, 1977).

Whitaker, Robert B. *A Plague on Both Your Houses* (Washington, D.C.: Robert B. Luce, Inc., 1976).

MAGAZINES

Bethell, Tom. "Fooling with the Budget," *Harper's Magazine*, October 1979.

Block, Julian. "Taxes: The Second American Revolution," *Argosy*, August 1979.

Business Week, October 23, 1978: "Inflationary Federal Pay Ripoff."

The Center Magazine, May–June 1978: "Taxation and Human Values."

Danziger, Sheldon, Haveman, Robert, and Plotnick, Robert, et al. "Poverty, Welfare, and Earnings: A New Approach," *Challenge*, September–October 1979.

Elgin, Duane, and Mitchell, Arnold. "Voluntary Simplicity," *CoEvolution Quarterly*, Summer 1977.

Epstein, Samuel S. "Cancer and the Environment," *Bulletin of the Atomic Scientists*, March 1977.

Gillette, Paul. "Will the Roof Cave in on California Housing?", *California Today*, April 1, 1979.

Industry Week, August 6, 1979: "Yankelovich on Today's Workers."

Journal of Taxation, January 1979: "Revenue Act of 1978 Makes Substantial Changes in the Taxation of Corporations."

King, Seth S. "Why Have One When Many Will Do?", *The New York Times Magazine,* September 16, 1979.

Miller, Arthur H. "Current Trends in Political Trust," *Economic Outlook USA,* Summer 1979.

Newsweek, October 1, 1979: "The Gold Rush of '79."

Schnee, Edward L., and Bates, Homer L. "Entertainment Expense Under the Revenue Act of 1978," *Taxes,* July 1979.

Speth, Gus. "A Small Price to Pay," *Environment,* October 1978.

Time, October 22, 1979: "The Squeeze of '79."

U.S. News & World Report, October 1, 1979: "Rocketing Inflation"; October 14, 1974: "Squeeze on America's Middle Class."; "New Breed of Workers," September 3, 1979.

NEWSPAPERS

Burham, J. B. "The Breakdown of Restraint," *Wall Street Journal,* October 3, 1979.

Diehl, Jackson. "Hogan Seeks to Outlaw Homes Under $85,000," *Washington Post,* September 30, 1979.

Edgerton, Michael. "Middle Managers: Guts of Organization," *Chicago Tribune,* October 14, 1979.

Elsner, David. "Executive Employment, Demand," *Chicago Tribune,* October 14, 1979.

Getler, Michael. "American Dream Blooms in Germany," *Washington Post,* August 29, 1979.

Greenberger, Robert S. "Unrelenting Inflation Deflates Many Hopes," *Wall Street Journal,* January 17, 1979.

Harris, Michael. "Little Things That Are Costing More," *San Francisco Chronicle,* April 27, 1979.

Herbers, John. "Nationwide Revolt on Taxes Showing No Signs of Abating," *New York Times,* August 5, 1979.

Los Angeles Times, September 2, 1979: "The American Struggle to Get Ahead in an Era of Inflation."

Mouat, Lucia. "Government Waste," *Christian Science Monitor,* May 24–June 1, 1976.

New York Times, September 11, 1979: "Alaska's Employees Quit Social Security."

San Francisco Chronicle, March 24, 1979: "Taxpayers Who Turn to Violence."

San Francisco Examiner, February 25, 1979: "Economic Facts of Life for Homebuyers."; September 30, 1979: "Home Prices Up $1,000 a Week."; February 3, 1980: "Home Sales Plunge, Prices Soar."

Sinclair, Ward. "The Race with Inflation: Win, Lose and Draw," *Washington Post*, December 12, 1979.

Washington Star, September 26, 1979: "Fraud at GSA Continues."

Yemma, John. "Social Welfare Still Getting Biggest Federal Budget Slice," *Christian Science Monitor*, January 1980.

Zwick, Charles J. "Federal Pay Scales Are Out of Sight," *New York Times*, March 4, 1979.

GOVERNMENT DOCUMENTS

(*Documents referred to generally are available from the Superintendent of Documents, U.S. Government Printing Office, Washington, D.C. 20402*)

Advisory Commission on Intergovernmental Relations: "Significant Features of Fiscal Federalism, 1978–1979," Washington, D.C., May 1979.

The Budget of the United States Government, Fiscal Years 1980 and 1981.

Bureau of the Census, U.S. Department of Commerce: "Money Income and Poverty Status of Families and Persons in the United States, 1978," Washington, D.C., November 1979.

Congressional Budget Office: "Growth of Government Spending for Income Assistance," December 1975; "Homeownership: The Changing Relationship of Costs and Incomes, and Possible Federal Roles," January 1977; "Federal White Collar Employees—Their Pay and Fringe Benefits," April 1979.

Danziger, Sheldon, Haveman, Robert, and Plotnick, Robert. "Income Transfer Programs in the United States" (prepared for the Joint Economic Committee, Congress of the United States; publication scheduled in 1980).

Executive Office of the President, Office of Management and Budget: *Improving Government Regulations,* Parts I and II, Washington, D.C., 1979.

Internal Revenue Service: *Internal Revenue Service, Statistics of Income— 1976, Individual Tax Returns,* Washington, D.C., 1979.

House of Representatives, Committee on Ways and Means, Ninety-fifth Congress, Second Session: Hearings, The President's 1978 Tax Program, March 14, 1978.

Joint Economic Committee, Congress of the United States: "How Public Welfare Benefits Are Distributed in Low-Income Areas," Washington, D.C., 1973.

President's Commission on Pension Policy: Proceedings, Detroit, Mich., October 24, 1979.

Office of Personnel Management: "Pay Structure of the Federal Civil Service," Washington, D.C., March 31, 1979.

"Special Analysis of the Budget of the United States Government, Fiscal Year 1980—Special Analysis F."

U.S. Department of Labor, Bureau of Labor Statistics: *Handbook of Labor Statistics 1978,* Washington, D.C., 1979.

SPEECHES

Austin, Penelope Canan. "The Federal Presence in Middletown, 1937–1977," Middletown III Project, presented to American Sociological Association, San Francisco, Calif., September 5, 1978.

Grace, J. Peter. "The Assault on Economic Incentive," remarks before the Symposium on American Capitalism, Fairfield University, March 19, 1980.

Yankelovich, Daniel. "New Approaches to Worker Productivity," presented to National Conference on Human Resource Systems, Dallas, Texas, October 25, 1978.

ASSOCIATION REPORTS

California Taxpayer's Association. "State Administrative Regulation in California," *Cal-Tax,* February 1, 1978.

Cagan, Phillip. "The Hydra-Headed Monster," American Enterprise Institute, Washington, D.C. 1976.

Citizen's Choice. "Big Government: Your Servant . . . Or Your Master?", Citizen's Choice, Washington, D.C. The author is grateful for this and other material supplied by Citizen's Choice, Inc., 1615 H Street NW, Washington, D.C. 20062.

Fuller, Robert. "Inflation: The Rising Cost of Living on a Small Planet," Worldwatch Institute Paper 34, Washington, D.C., January 1980.

Nulty, Leslie Ellen. "Understanding the New Inflation: The Importance of the Basic Necessities," Exploratory Project for Economic Alternatives, Washington, D.C., 1977. The author is grateful for this and other materials furnished by the National Center for Economic Alternatives and its affiliated group, Citizens Opposed to Inflation in the Necessities, both located in Washington, D.C.

Pascal, Anthony H., et al. "Fiscal Containment of Local and State Government," Rand Corporation, Santa Monica, Calif., September 1979.

—— and Menchik, Mark David. "Fiscal Containment: Who Gains? Who Loses?", Rand Corporation, September 1979.

Towers, Perrin, Forster & Crosby. "Worldwide Total Remuneration," New York, 1979.

DISSERTATIONS AND WORKS IN PROGRESS

Caplow, Theodore, "The Changing Middletown Family," Middletown III Project, September 1, 1979.

—— and Bahr, Howard. "Half a Century of Change in Adolescent Attitudes: Replication of a Middletown Survey by the Lynds," Middletown III Project, 1978.

Hong, Byung Yoo. "Inflation Under Cost Pass-Along Management," Ph.D. dissertation, Columbia University, 1978.

Rosow, Jerome M. "The Middle Age Bulge," draft article, Fall 1979.

APPENDIX

A FURTHER NOTE ON PRICES AND INCOMES

A. PRICES

People in [White House] *meetings are really talking about hyperinflation.*—Carter Administration aide, *Time,* March 10, 1980.

By the middle of 1923, the whole of Germany had become delirious. Whoever had a job got paid every day, usually at noon, and then ran to the nearest store, with a sack full of banknotes, to buy anything he could get, at any price. In their frenzy, people paid millions and even billions of marks for cuckoo clocks, shoes that didn't fit, anything that could be traded for something else . . . "The collapse of the currency not only meant the end of trade, bankrupt businesses, food shortages in the big cities and unemployment," according to one historian, Alan Bullock. "It had the effect, which is the unique quality of economic catastrophe, of reaching down to and touching every single member of the community in a way which no political event can."—Otto Friedrich, in *Before the Deluge.*

In August 1922, the German money supply stood at 252 billion marks. Four months later it was two trillion marks. In September 1923, Germany's grotesquely inflated economy was being fueled by twenty-eight quadrillion marks, and in November the figure reached 497 quintillion. Germans were paying more than a billion marks for a single loaf of bread. To provide relief for its legions of idled industrial workers, the desperate Reichsbank requisitioned newspaper presses to print more worthless currency. "The fundamental quality of the disaster," wrote Otto Friedrich, "was a complete loss of faith in the functioning of society."

Could that kind of devastating inflation happen again? Indeed, hyperinflation has appeared more than once in the current century. Though soon controlled, runaway prices raged through much of Europe after World War II. For years, inflation in Brazil ranged from 20

183

to 50 per cent annually. Two of the world's present day economies—Israel and Argentina, where annual price increases during the 1970s reached or neared 100 per cent—have experienced runaway inflation rates. Indonesia, Great Britain and Yugoslavia are other nations where double-digit inflation was consistently experienced throughout the 1970s. But that still doesn't tell us whether true runaway inflation could occur here.

At least as frustrating, no one seems quite prepared to say what runaway inflation actually is. At what point does the "ordinary" inflation most non-Communist nations experienced since World War II become something far more ominous, that salivating beast of economics, hyperinflation? Official definitions of runaway inflation are hard to come by, partly because America has little historial experience with hyperinflation, and partly because politicians, especially those who have encouraged inflationary policies, are frightened of the topic. Moreover, periodic recessions have helped mask over the fact that prices were still rising, albeit at a slower rate.

General agreement exists, however, that runaway inflation has begun if, for a prolonged period, the increase in money income fails to keep up with price inflation by a substantial margin. Until then, inflation is apt to be wearing the attractive disguise of prosperity. At times during the 1970s and early 1980s, the U.S. edged close to the starting line of hyperinflation. Twice, in 1974–1975 and again at the end of the Seventies, real incomes went into actual decline. To be more precise:

- In 1979, the last year of what some economists were calling "the inflation decade," American private sector workers lost $1 a day in buying power—despite wage increases averaging over 7 per cent.

- In 10 years inflation had chopped 50 cents from the 1970 dollar. Importantly, the steady drop was not halted by the recession of the mid-1970s, the most severe economic downturn since the Great Depression.

- While prices were shooting out of sight, the median real income of American families advanced through most of the "inflation decade" at well under 1 per cent annually. In contrast, according to Census Bureau figures, real median family incomes rose by nearly 40 per cent during the 1950s and more than 30 per cent in the 1960s. In four of the eight

184

years of the Eisenhower Administration, it should be mentioned, prices rose by less than 1 per cent.

Contrast those happier days with the analysis of J. Peter Grace, chairman of W. R. Grace & Co. To show the state of the U.S. economy as the 1980s arrived, Grace examined six key economic indicators from the recent past, compiling a chilling portrait of how much the economy had worsened in little more than a decade.

THE DETERIORATING U.S. ECONOMY

	6 Years Ending			% (Deterior- ation) 1968–1979
	1968	1973	1979	
(1) Real GNP (Avg. Ann. % Change)	4.7%	3.4%	2.5%	(46.8)%
(2) Unemployment Rate (Avg. %)	4.4	4.7	6.8	(54.5)
(3) Productivity (Avg. Ann. % Change)	3.4	2.1	0.6	(82.4)
(4) Real Business Investment (Avg. Ann. % Change)	7.3	4.0	2.1	(71.2)
(5) Inflation (Avg. Ann. % Change)	2.4	4.9	8.5	(254.2)
(6) Federal Deficit (Avg., $ Billions)	$(3.9)	$(9.2)	$(36.6)	(838.5)

Inflation was far and away the most pernicious of our economic ills. As the Council of Economic Advisers observed several years ago: "The inflation came in various forms—sometimes led by wages, sometimes by prices, by food, by oil; sometimes it was domestic and sometimes imported. Many programs have been launched to stop it—without durable success. Inflation seemed a hydra-headed monster, growing two new heads each time one was cut off." The new decade saw the same pattern repeated. After a historic rise, by May, 1980, mortgage rates finally began to drop. Within days, however, another key

185

component of consumer prices—fossil fuels—took a big jump, when Saudi Arabia raised the price of oil by $2 a barrel.

Not only was inflation many-faceted, it was sustained, even in the face of recession. "The distinctive feature of the postwar inflations has not been that prices rose faster in periods of cyclical expansion," wrote Columbia economist Phillip Cagan, "but that they declined hardly at all, or even rose, in recessions." Indeed, in the four decades following 1940, prices in the U.S. actually fell significantly only twice—in 1949 and 1955. It may be worthwhile to glance at a graphic display of U.S. consumer prices through the nation's history.

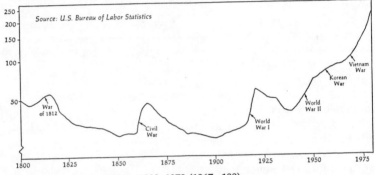

U.S. Consumer Price Index, 1800–1979 (1967=100)

The most immediate observation is the steep upward slope of the line at the right side of the graph—never in our history has a price rise been as prolonged as now. But there is another part of this graph that should be noticed as a caution against overreacting against inflation. That is the long trough of *de*flation extending through the last quarter of the nineteenth century and almost up to World War I.

Virtually from the time of the Civil War on, the nation was locked in debate over "sound money." The southern and western sections of the country, historically in debt to eastern banks, wanted easy money, which in those days meant increased coinage of silver as well as paper money. The eastern establishment argued for conservative financial policies and eventually won out, at least partly because the runaway inflations during and just after the Revolutionary War remained a vivid memory. Even during the Civil War, when the government issued "greenbacks" to meet its obligations, paper currency fluctuated vio-

186

lently—at one point the greenbacks were exchanged for a gold price of as little as 35 cents on the dollar. So the nation overreacted, following tight money policies which not only added to the burdens of the farmers and unemployed, but also may well have limited business expansion.

The lesson is that once prudence is abandoned, the cure for inflation can be as painful as the disease itself. "Inflation is the only politically feasible way that democratic governments have found for allocating increased real costs," writes Robert Fuller of the Worldwatch Institute. By the same token, the clumsy tools of unemployment and high interest rates, have been the only way to slow inflation down. Since those devices are never politically acceptable for very long, the cycle is almost guaranteed to be self-perpetuating.

In the end the most meaningful gauge of the effect of rising prices is probably found in our everyday lives. Take wine, for example. The *average* price increase among 59 fine varietal wines recommended by *The Wine Investor*, a newsletter for wine collectors and industry insiders, was 100 per cent over a three-year period. Even more basic to the national palate has been the sharp escalation in food costs. And nothing could have made that point more sharply than a fifteenth anniversary party staged by an Oakland, California, restaurant late in 1979. In honor of the occasion, and to thank its loyal customers, the eatery rolled back its prices to 1964 levels. The relatively small restaurant, a popular fish establishment called "The Ark," was mobbed by local television crews and patrons who waited nearly three hours for a table. When finally seated, those who survived the crush opened their menus to discover shocking evidence of just how much prices had risen in a decade and a half:

From the Galley

THE ARK'S own recipe Fisherman Style **CLAM CHOWDER** Large .40 Small .25

SEAFOOD COCKTAILS
Served supreme with THE ARK'S own spicy sauce

LOBSTER MEAT .90	CRAB MEAT .90	COMBINATION Lobster, Shrimp, Crab .80	SHRIMP MEAT .75	EASTERN OYSTER .90

SUPREME SALADS
fresh-tossed with our famous dressing. Choice of Roquefort or Anchovy served with crackers.

CRAB
Supreme, Reg.	1.25
Supreme, Small	.85
Crab, Louie	1.75
Small	1.00
With Louie Dressing

SHRIMP
Supreme, Reg.	1.15
Supreme, Small	.75
Shrimp, Louie	1.25
Small	.85
With Louie Dressing

LOBSTER
Supreme, Reg.	1.60
Supreme, Small	1.10
Lobster, Louie	1.85
Small	1.35
With Louie Dressing

COMBINATIONS
Supreme, Reg.	1.55
Supreme, Small	1.00
Comb., Louie	1.65
Small	1.25
With Louie Dressing

SANDWICHES
ABALONE	. . .	.90
CLUB HOUSE	. .	1.50
Turkey, Tomato, Bacon		
CRAB SALAD	. .	.75
BEEFBURGER	. .	.85
We grind our own
French Fries, Pickles, Olives

STEAK SANDWICH
Choice Top Sirloin
French Fries, Dinner Salad
2.00

SCATTER SHRIMP
A platter of tiny Golden Fried Shrimp, French Fries, Cole Slaw
1.50

CLAMS
Plain, Steamed, Drawn Butter, Cup of Broth
1.70

FRIED CHICKEN	with Cole Slaw	. .	1.60
FISH 'N' CHIPS	with Hush Puppies*	.	1.35
ABALONE 'N' CHIPS	with Hush Puppies*		1.60
FRIED PRAWNS	with Hush Puppies*	.	1.10
SCALLOPS 'N' CHIPS	with Hush Puppies*		1.55

TOP SIRLOIN
With Lobster Tail
Salad, French Fries French Bread
3.95

LOBSTER
Broiled Australian Lobster Tails
Served with Salad, French Fries, Drawn Butter, French Bread
3.25

FRESH CRACKED CRAB
In Season
Whole — 2.00
Half — 1.25

CHILDREN'S PLATE
Children's Portions Served on the Above Entrees
15¢ Less than prices listed

CAPTAIN'S PLATE
Combination of Seafood.
Oyster, Prawns, Abalone, Fish.
French Fries, Hush Puppies*
1.75

OYSTERS
Deep Fried
Eastern Oysters
1.55

GARLIC BREAD
.35

Coffee	. . .	.15			
Iced Coffee	. . .	.15	SHERBET	. .	.25
Sanka	. .	.15	ICE CREAM	.	.25

CHEESE CAKE .	.40
CHOC. SUNDAE .	.35

Tea, per cup	. .	.15
Iced Tea, Coffee	.	.15
Milk .	. . .	.15

*"Hush-Puppies belong to Georgia fish fries. The tale is that once upon a time at a fish fry the dogs on the plantation set up such a howl for fish that some cornbread batter was dropped into the hot grease in which the fish had been fried, and when done it was thrown to the dogs to quiet them. The dogs gulped them with such relish and howled for more that a guest tasted them and howled for more too. From that time on, Hush-Puppies were a specialty of the house at fish fries."

We try to prevent loss, but cannot assume responsibility for lost articles.

Please allow sufficient time to properly prepare each individual order.

All menu items prepared to to take out.

B. INCOMES

It may be helpful to extend briefly the discussion of incomes raised in the opening newsreel, "The Troubled Middle." As the *Congressional Quarterly* observed in 1978, middle income Americans "actually are poorer than many of the definitions of middle income used in Congress." Congressional definitions, the magazine continued, place the middle class between levels as low as $10,000 or $15,000 and as high as $30,000 or even $50,000. "In fact," reported *CQ*, "the majority of Americans have incomes at the low end of that range and below."

Adjusting *CQ* figures upward to reflect average national wage increases in 1978 and 1979, yields a middle-income range of $16,830 to $28,965, if middle is defined as the middle one-third of all Americans. Under a broader definition in which half the wage-earning population is assumed to be middle income, the range is $15,341 to $32,286. Fully a third of the nation's households have incomes below $10,000, according to Census Bureau data published late in 1979 (based on 1978 income estimates); another 25 per cent, many of them in the "working poor" category, fall between $12,000 and $20,000 annually. Only 12 per cent had incomes in the $30,000 to $40,000 range and less than 3 per cent of the nation's families were above $50,000.

There is something else worth noting about the characteristics of American households. Over three-fourths of the non-dependent adult population are married persons living under one roof. As we have seen earlier, the majority of households with incomes above $25,000 are two-paycheck husband-wife couples. What if the non-married population continues to grow faster than those who are married? A good guess is that family incomes will decline. That's because wives returning to work were the single most important factor in keeping family budgets afloat throughout the inflation of the 1970s. Without them, the question of "who is middle class?" could become academic.

INDEX

191

194